Contents

Acknowledgements   iv
Series Editor's Preface   vii
Introduction   viii

Case 1 Alhambra Bingo Clubs   1
    New audit: procedures and planning

Case 2 Elliott Transmitters plc   7
    Systems controls and weaknesses: flowcharting

Case 3 Green Fingers Limited   16
    Audit of a small company

Case 4 Esparto Limited   36
    Analytical review in audit planning

Case 5 The Enormous Electrical Company   44
    Audit of a stocktake

Case 6 Technical Wizardry Limited   48
    Audit of a stock valuation

Case 7 Warehousemasters Limited   53
    Audit of debtors

Case 8 Britlings Brewery   61
    Fixed assets: systems and substantive tests

Case 9 Mrs Beeton's Kitchens Limited   67
    Purchases system: audit of creditors and accruals

Case 10 Golden Foods Limited   73
    Resolving audit problem areas

Case 11 Massive Motors Limited 78
Post balance-sheet events, commitments, contingencies

Case 12 Holiday Holdings Limited 84
Analytical review as a direct test of balances

Case 13 Fantasy Fashions Limited 87
Audit reports: stock valuation

Case 14 Brighter Alloys Limited 92
Fraud

Case 15 Banbury Group plc 101
The auditor and going concern

Solution Notes 109
Bibliography 166

CASES

W·CH

Josephine Maltby is a chartered accountant. She worked for Ernst & Young as a senior audit manager before taking up her present post as a lecturer in accounting at Sheffield University Management School.

CASES IN AUDITING

JOSEPHINE MALTBY
Sheffield University Management School

P·C·P
Paul Chapman
Publishing Ltd

Acknowledgements

I should like to thank the following people for their assistance with this book:

David Stephens of Ernst & Young and David Starr of Grant Thornton, who kindly designed and provided me with material which I have used in the following cases:

Ernst & Young:
Elliott Transmitters plc
Green Fingers Limited
Esparto Limited

Grant Thornton:
Holiday Holdings Limited.

R. A. Rickson of Extel Financial, 37–45 Paul Street, London EC2A 4PB for permission to use material from a card compiled by Extel Financial in the case of the Banbury Group plc.

Mike Hayes and Bill Speirs of Sheffield University Management School for advice in compling the Brighter Alloys Limited case.

Valerie Patrick for her assistance in preparing the manuscript of this book.

Marianne Lagrange and Catherine Blishen of Paul Chapman Publishing for their advice, enthusiasm and encouragement.

First published 1991
Paul Chapman Publishing Ltd
144 Liverpool Road
LONDON N1 1LA

British Library Cataloguing in Publication Data

Maltby, Josephine
  Cases in auditing.
  1. Auditing
  I. Title
  657.45

ISBN 1 85396 068 3

Typeset by Setrite, Hong Kong
Printed in Great Britain by Hollen Street Press Ltd, Slough

A B C D E F G H I 8 7 6 5 4 3 2 1

Series Editor's Preface

It is often said that the best way to learn about auditing practice is through the experience of doing the job. Indeed, there is probably no substitute for the time spent 'in the field' trying to glean information about the sales system or evaluating the value of stock in the balance sheet.

However, it is not feasible, nor is it desirable, for all auditing education and training to be gained on the job. In the first place there is a body of theoretical knowledge that underlies auditing practice which also has to be learnt and critically evaluated. Secondly, students of auditing are required to take examinations in the subject during, and even before the commencement of, their audit work experience. Therefore, a wide variety of written teaching materials are needed both to complement and to substitute the practical experience gained in the audit firm. The theories and principles that underlie auditing practice are discussed in textbooks which emphasize the conceptual basis of auditing, two of which, *Auditing and Accountability* and *Current Issues in Auditing*, are published in this series. The current standards and guidelines are to be found in the official publications of the professional accountancy bodies and the more practically oriented textbooks and tutors' manuals. To complement these texts and to provide an alternative to experience in the field it is therefore necessary to make use of a case study book containing examples of actual audit situations.

It is this last role that this new book by Josephine Maltby, *Cases in Auditing*, so admirably fills. Based on her professional auditing experience she has prepared fifteen original case studies. Each case study addresses a different audit issue and requires the student to assess the evidence available, to determine whether and what additional audit work should be undertaken, and to exercise their judgement on the reliability of the financial statements.

Cases in Auditing, uniquely amongst auditing case books, includes suggested solutions at the end of the book. Although by no means a definitive answer to the problems raised in the case study, this feature means that the book may be used both as a basis for classroom discussion and as part of a self-learning programme. As a result, *Cases in Auditing* is an indispensable learning aid both for undergraduate students taking an auditing course as part of an accounting degree and for students taking professional auditing examinations. I am sure that Josephine Maltby's highly readable and very useful book will soon become the standard by which other auditing case study books are judged and I am delighted that it is included in this series.

Michael J. Sherer
University of Essex

Introduction

The aim of this book is to act as a supplement, and perhaps sometimes a corrective, to the auditing texts in current use in undergraduate and professional courses. Texts such as Woolf (1990) and Coopers & Lybrand (1985) are deservedly included on students' reading lists. They give a thorough account of the requirements of the auditing standards and guidelines and of the way in which these should be implemented in different audit areas. The student is given a clear and comprehensive overview of the auditing process, from planning via testing to the final audit opinion, together with detailed suggestions for the kind of tests which are appropriate to different audit areas.

The disadvantage of studying auditing through these and similar texts is that they outline the procedures to be followed but give the student little idea of what happens when these procedures have to be applied to a real situation. Auditing appears to be the more or less mechanical performance of a number of predetermined steps – a duller, but also a much less problematical activity than it actually is.

Cases in Auditing has been written with the intention of introducing students to the problems that arise in applying auditing standards and guidelines in practice.

The case study format was adopted because, in the words of Easton (1982, p. 5), 'The case method is primarily a vehicle for developing skills'. Easton identifies six major skills which can be developed by the case method: analytical, application, creative, communication, social and self-analysis skills. Two of these skills – analysis and application – are particularly relevant to the teaching of auditing. This may be illustrated by considering the role of evidence in auditing.

Sherer and Kent (1983, pp. 51–2) stress the fundamental importance of evidence to the audit process, but also state clearly the problems that face the auditor in identifying and evaluating audit evidence:

> the concept of evidence in auditing is far less well defined than it is in law. In a court of law experts represent each side and have a duty to make a case by presenting all the evidence which they can: to regulate the procedure there are well defined rules concerning admissibility, and the final decision as to relevance and validity is made by the judge and jury.
>
> This is not the case with respect to auditing. There are no rules of admissibility. The auditor has access to an enormous amount of existing evidence in the form of the company's books and records and can obtain more from the company's officials, his [sic] own efforts and third parties. He must recognize that which is not relevant and discard it; he must recognize that which is relevant and accord it its due weight in his considerations.

Cases in Auditing attempts to introduce students to the problems presented by what Hatherley (1980) calls the audit evidence process, and thereby to develop their analytical skills. Each case contains data in various forms, including systems descriptions, financial statements and extracts from accounting records, notes of meetings and discussions and the results of audit tests. The student is required to analyse the data in order to:

1. identify potential problem areas;
2. identify those parts of the data which constitute relevant audit evidence;
3. determine how complete and reliable that evidence is.

Not all the information contained in the case will be relevant to the problem; sometimes the conclusions drawn from it by the auditor will be invalid. The student will need to use judgement to assess the evidence available and determine how it might be supplemented by other audit work.

Application skills are closely linked to analytical ones. Analysis is needed to identify the problem and the relevant evidence; the next step is for the auditor to determine which audit tests are appropriate in the circumstances. This is not simply a matter of enumerating all the tests possible on a given audit area. Certain tests may not be possible for a number of reasons. A client's system may be defective or non-existent, so that controls are not there to be tested. Time pressures may make other types of testing impossible – for instance, if the audit deadline comes very close to the year-end. Fee pressures may have an impact on the work done; the auditor will have to ensure that only the most cost-effective tests are performed, so that there is inevitably some trade-off between time taken and degree of assurance obtained.

Analysis and application combine in devising an audit approach that is tailor-made to a specific situation. The student has to determine both what audit work is necessary and what is possible, given the constraints that exist.

HOW TO USE THIS BOOK

The cases in this book are intended to cover all stages in the audit, from the inception of a new engagement to the clearance of outstanding matters. They are of varying length and difficulty, but there is no ascending order of complexity.

The cases can be tackled either by a student working alone or by groups of students preparing the work in advance for a class discussion. Most cases are too long to be dealt with from scratch in an hour's tutorial. The solution notes contain the following information.

1. A brief summary of the material the case is intended to cover: this will not be exhaustive, in that it is impossible to test one aspect of the audit process completely in isolation. For instance, a case dealing with the audit of stocks will draw upon such areas as audit planning, systems testing and substantive testing in general.

2. Suggested readings: these are based principally on auditing standards and guidelines and on two texts − Woolf (1990) and Coopers & Lybrand (1985). Teachers may wish to suggest other readings from texts they are using − for instance Gray and Manson (1989) − or to refer students to relevant portions of their lectures.
3. Suggested solution: there is no one correct solution to any of the cases. The suggested solution represents an attempt to respond to all the factors in the case study, but students may well arrive at other answers based on their own evaluation of the problem. What is important is that students should attempt to arrive at a solution that is responsive to the facts of the individual case.

The student working alone would be best advised to jot down an outline of the case after reading it once or twice, and then to proceed to the first part of the suggested solution, i.e. the section on subject matter. This will enable the student to confirm that he or she has correctly identified the problem to be addressed. He or she should then refer to the passages listed under 'Relevant reading', as these will contain the relevant technical material, and will help the student to consider the problem in greater depth, and will suggest ways of tackling it.

Case 1
Alhambra Bingo Clubs

BACKGROUND

Gwynn & Co. is a small firm of chartered accountants in Cardiff. The audit partner has been asked to make a proposal to Alhambra Bingo Clubs (ABC), a Cardiff-based company, which wants to change from its present auditors.

PEOPLE INVOLVED

Gwynn & Co.
Ron Dare (RD): Senior Partner
Louise Gordon (LG): Audit Partner
Tim West (TW): Audit Senior

Alhambra Bingo Clubs
Simon Kramer (SK): Financial Director
Peter Foley (PF): Accountant

DOCUMENTS

1.1 Gwynn & Co. – Memorandum

From   RD
To   LG   *7 January 19X8*

Louise
I was introduced to Simon Kramer at the golf club on Saturday. He is a director of Alhambra Bingo Clubs. His father, Jack, is the MD and gradually retiring from active involvement with the company. I get the impression that Howells, who are ABC's present auditors, were Jack's choice and Simon fancies a change to somebody a bit more dynamic. They haven't fallen out with Howells, but I gather that Simon wants advice about computerizing ABC's system, which Howells can't provide.

Simon has asked us to make a proposal. Would you like to go and see him to glean a bit of information about the company?

Ron

1

1.2 Gwynn & Co. – Memorandum

From   LG

To   TW   *9 January 19X8*

Tim

I've made an appointment to see the financial director of ABC on 13 Jan. Will you come along too, please, and interview the financial accountant, Peter Foley? We need to assemble as much information as possible about ABC's business and systems so that we can plan the audit in outline.

LG

1.3 Extract from note of a meeting with Simon Kramer at ABC's offices on 13 January 19X8

I asked SK to give me a potted history of ABC. He explained that it was formed in the 1920s and had initially owned a chain of cinemas in South Wales. Jack began converting them to bingo halls in the 1960s and also acquired a couple of clubs from other operators. There are now 15 ABC clubs, all in Wales and the West of England.

Simon is planning a major acquisition. A company in Bristol has contacted ABC to ask whether they are interested in acquiring 6 clubs in that area which will be put on the market in July this year. ABC will need a bank loan of about £250k to finance the purchase and the bank will want to see up-to-date audited accounts to support the application. SK stressed that the audit must therefore be completed by 1 July at the latest. (This may give us problems, as ABC's year-end is 31 May and we are normally fairly busy in June. I didn't mention this to Simon, though.)

Simon isn't involved in day-to-day accounting. He leaves that to Peter Foley, who is unqualified but very experienced and has been with ABC for 7 years. I got the impression that the accounting staff are under a lot of pressure. As the number of clubs has increased, Peter and his staff have become increasingly snowed under with work. The club managers 'aren't recruited on their book-keeping ability' (according to SK) and they can be quite slapdash about making returns. Peter spends a lot of time chasing them for overdue information. A computer would definitely help, but nobody in the company has much idea of what to buy. Simon confirmed that, if we are appointed, he would like us to advise them about systems improvements in general and computerization in particular.

He also mentioned that Howells gave ABC assistance in preparing the statutory accounts, and were responsible for the company's tax computation. He would like us to take over these functions ...

We agreed that I would send him a proposal, setting out the likely level of our fees and the service we can offer.

1.4   ABC – Organization chart

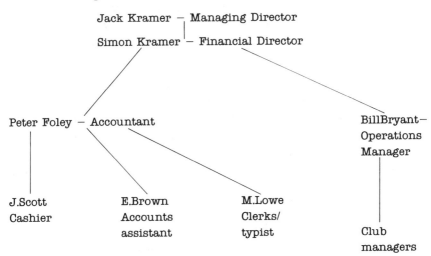

Jack Kramer – Managing Director

Simon Kramer – Financial Director

Peter Foley – Accountant

BillBryant– Operations Manager

J.Scott Cashier

E.Brown Accounts assistant

M.Lowe Clerks/ typist

Club managers

1.5   ABC Ltd – Brief systems notes

Prepared by TW   *13.1.X8*

There are 3 main activities at the clubs – bingo games, gaming (i.e. 'fruit') machines and café sales.

BINGO   *Clubs have 2 sessions daily – afternoon and evening. Members pay an admission fee and then so much per bingo card. Most of the card price (less gaming duty) is paid out again as prize money.*

Cards issued are sequentially numbered and all numbers have to be accounted for by club management. This is a control to ensure that all proceeds from card sales are received by the company.

ABC is required to keep detailed records of games played for gaming duty purposes. Club managers make a weekly return to head office of cards sold and cash taken.

GAMING MACHINES   *ABC rents all its gaming machines from Havago Ltd. A Havago collector visits each club once a week, unlocks and empties each machine and hands over the takings to the club manager, less £20 rent. The collector fills in a return showing the amount of the takings and sends a copy to ABC's head office (HO).*

CAFÉ SALES   *A till is installed in each café. Managers send till rolls to HO each week, together with a summary of takings.*

HO accounts staff collate the club returns, review them for possible errors and discrepancies and enter the weekly totals in the nominal ledger.

BANK & CASH ACCOUNTS   *Managers are responsible for banking cash. They send the paying-in slips to HO. Each club has a petty cash float of a set amount − £100 to £250, depending on club size. Managers record payments in a club petty cash book. They are allowed to use cash from takings to reimburse the float.*

There is one bank account, controlled by HO. All cheques must be signed by a director. Club managers have no access to the bank account. The cashier writes up the cash book, using the paying-in data received from clubs, and prepares a monthly bank reconciliation.

PURCHASES   *Apart from petty cash purchases, all goods and services are paid for by HO. Managers approve purchase invoices by signing them and then send them to HO for payment. HO enters them in the purchase ledger and sends cheques directly to suppliers.*

Apparently there was a problem last year-end as some managers were late in sending in purchase invoices relating to purchases before the year-end and creditors were understated as a result.

FIXED ASSETS   *The main tangible ones are the freeholds of 4 clubs (Swansea, Swindon, Hereford and Cardiff; the other clubs are leasehold) and the newly installed fixtures and fittings at Swansea and Hereford. Equipment in the other clubs in largely fully depreciated.*

STOCK   *This is mainly canteen supplies and stationery − bingo cards and tickets. Club managers do a count every month.*

GENERAL   *PF and his staff seem efficient but are clearly under pressure in dealing with all the returns they get from clubs.*

PF commented that he expects to see a lot of the auditors again this year. Apparently Howells normally spend several weeks checking from the club returns to the nominal ledger. They also counted cash and took stock at all the clubs during the week after the year-end.

1.6   ABC Ltd − Summarized accounts for the year ended 31.5.X7

	£m
Turnover	2.4
Expenses:	
Wages	0.9
Clubs (rent, rates, light & heat etc.)	0.5
Depreciation	0.1
HO (salaries, legal &	0.3
professional etc.)	—
Profit before tax	0.6
Taxation	0.2

Retained profit	0.4

Fixed assets	2.0
	—
Stock	0.1
Bank	0.2
Cash	0.2

	0.5

Creditors	0.6
Net assets	1.9
	—
Share capital	1.0
Retained profits	0.9
	1.9
	—

1.7 Summary of branch results for the year ended 31.5.X7

(All £000)

BRANCH		Turnover	Club expenses	Cash at year-end	Stock at year-end
1	Abergavenny	165	50	25	9
2	Cardiff	360	60	30	13
3	Cheltenham	180	35	11	10
4	Fishguard	55	12	5	1
5	Hereford	115	29	10	1
6	Llanelli	180	60	15	5
7	Monmouth	100	24	7	6
8	Neath	85	13	8	7
9	Newport	170	40	15	12
10	Porthcawl	75	16	5	2
11	Port Talbot	260	46	17	3
12	Swansea	255	40	20	11
13	Swindon	130	22	10	4
14	Tenby	95	23	8	10
15	Weston	175	30	14	6
		2400	500	200	100

QUESTIONS FOR DISCUSSION

1. Assume that ABC's directors accept Gwynn & Co.'s proposal. What steps must Gwynn & Co. now take? Suggest the contents of any letters they will need to write.
2. Prepare a plan for the 19X8 audit. It should cover:
   (a) the timing of the audit;
   (b) locations to be visited;
   (c) nature of audit tests to be performed;
   (d) any possible problem areas.

Relevant reading

Auditing Practices Committee (1989a):
   Auditing Standards: 1.101   The auditor's operational standard
   Auditing Guidelines: 4.406   The engagement letter
ICAEW (1979)
Woolf (1990), pp. 47–69
Lee (1986), pp. 57–66

Case 2
Elliott Transmitters plc

BACKGROUND

Elliott Transmitters (ET) imports and sells special telephone equipment such as portable telephones and car phones and also walkie-talkies. Its customers include chain stores, mail order companies and wholesalers. ET's year-end is 31 December. It is early July and the audit team is carrying out the interim audit for the 1989 year-end. The senior in charge of the interim audit has prepared an audit planning memorandum, which sets out the salient features of ET's business and performance in the past twelve months.

DOCUMENTS

2.1 Extract from audit planning memorandum

SALES AND DEBTORS

Latest figures (unaudited)

	6 months to 30.6.89 £000	Year ended 31.12.88 £000
Gross sales	1,677	3,518
	------	------
Trade debtors	507	467
Doubtful debt provision	(5)	(5)
	------	------
	502	462
	------	------

ET has about 275 customers. The average debt collection period is 7 weeks. In the past, ET has had very few bad debts; the total write-off for the year ended 31 December 1988 was less than £2,000. The company attributes this to the intensive credit investigations to which it subjects prospective customers. Customers must have their creditworthiness checked by a commercial agency before they are allowed credit. They are then assigned a credit limit; ET refuses to supply goods if this would take them over the limit. Each month, the computer produces an aged list of ledger balances. All customers who are overdue (i.e. with balances over 30 days old) are sent a reminder letter.

STOCKS

ET carries about 45 different lines in stock. All movements of stock are shown on a monthly stock ledger print-out produced by the computer. The company has a physical count of major stock lines monthly and all stock at the year-end. Stocks at 30.6.89 were £554k (31.12.88 £494k). There appear to have been some large stock losses which came to light during the June stocktake. These are still being investigated.

ACCOUNTING SYSTEM: CHANGES SINCE LAST YEAR

The company has recently introduced a small computer into the sales system. Despatch notes are produced manually and input to the computer. It then produces invoices, posts them to the books of account and prints summaries and reports at the end of the month.

2.2 Detailed analytical review (extracts)

£000	TURNOVER 1989	
	BUDGET	*ACTUAL*
Jan	*300*	*276*
Feb	*340*	*325*
Mar	*330*	*280*
Apr	*350*	*267*
May	*310*	*265*
Jun	*300*	*264*
	1,930	*1,677*

%	GROSS MARGIN	
Jan	*25*	*24*
Feb	*26*	*27*
Mar	*24*	*25*
Apr	*25*	*23*
May	*26*	*31*
Jun	*25*	*19*

I discussed the fluctuations in gross margin with the assistant accountant, Sally Green. She stated that the sharp drop in margin in June is thought to be possibly the result of stock losses. The company is currently investigating the position.

2.3 Organization chart

The personnel involved in the sales system are:

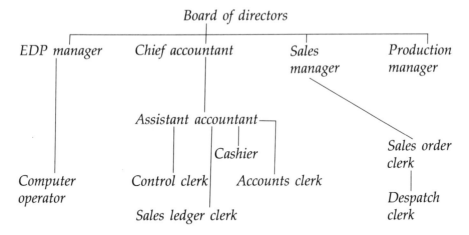

2.4 Transcript of an interview with sales manager

John Vaz (V), an audit trainee, interviewed Judith Andrews (A), the sales manager, as a preliminary to documenting the sales system. The conversation went as follows:

V I believe all the sales orders are received and processed here: is that right?

A Yes.

V Good. Shall we start with the receipt of a customer's order? How do you receive these? Do they come in by post or telephone or fax?

A Mostly on the customer's own order form. We sometimes get telephone orders, but then we insist they are confirmed in writing by the customer. Anyway, we immediately transfer the order on to our own sales order form and work out the value. Then we use the internal form to check whether the item is in stock. If it is, we mark the sales order form accordingly.

V What then?

A We make out an order confirmation for those items that we have in stock and note on the bottom of the confirmation the items which are either out of stock or not quickly obtainable. If none of the items ordered is in stock then I write a rejection letter giving the reason. I compare the customer order with our sales order and the confirmation. Then I sign the confirmation and send it off. We file the sales order with the original order.

V How are they filed?

A In customer account number order.

V Where do you get the number from?

A Oh, I forgot to mention that! Mary, the sales order clerk, puts it on the sales order when we have checked that the customer is within his credit limit.

V When and how do you do that check?

A I suppose that's the first thing we do, really. It's so automatic I forgot about it. As soon as we've priced the sales order, Mary examines the aged analysis of debtors in the accounts department. She looks at the current balance and compares it with the credit limit. If she sees that the customer has an account and is within his limit, she enters his account number on the order.

V What if he doesn't already have an account?

A We ask a credit rating agency to investigate his creditworthiness. If they write to say that his credit is good, I enter customer details, account number and credit limit on a sales ledger master file amendment form. Then I file the letter on the customer master file. I send the master file amendment form to data processing for input to the computer. If I didn't approve the account, we would send a rejection letter and file it with the copy letter and the rejected order. This would be alphabetically filed by customer name.

V Is there any procedure for reviewing credit limits?

A How do you mean?

V I mean checking whether a customer should be given a lower level of credit, if his financial position worsened, for instance.

A No, we don't do that.

V Let's see now; you said an order confirmation was made out after you'd checked on stock availability. How many copies of the confirmation are there?

A There are 4 copies in pre-numbered sets.

V And what happens to them?

A The top copy goes to the customer. We send the second copy to the despatch department who use it to select the goods and make up the order. The third copy goes to the sales ledger clerk and Mary files the fourth in alphabetical order by customer name.

V Do you check the price quoted by the customer on the original order?

A No. Our terms of sale are that goods will be invoiced at the price ruling on the date of delivery.

V Fine. I think that's told me what I need to know about the process for accepting orders. Thanks for your help.

2.5 Flowchart: procedure for making up and despatching orders

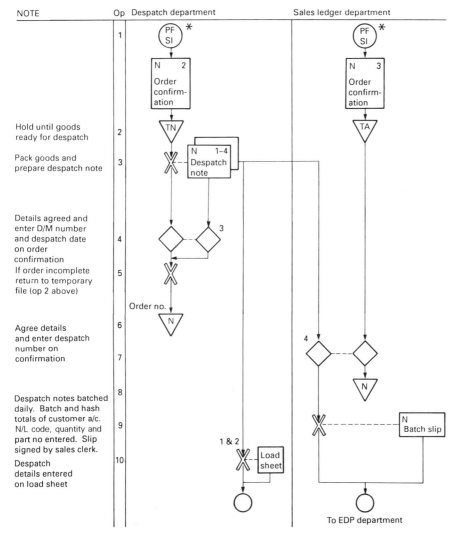

ELLIOTT TRANSMITTERS
Procedures for despatching orders

* Refers to an earlier part of the file which charted
  the process for taking orders

ELLIOT TRANSMITTERS
Procedures for despatching orders

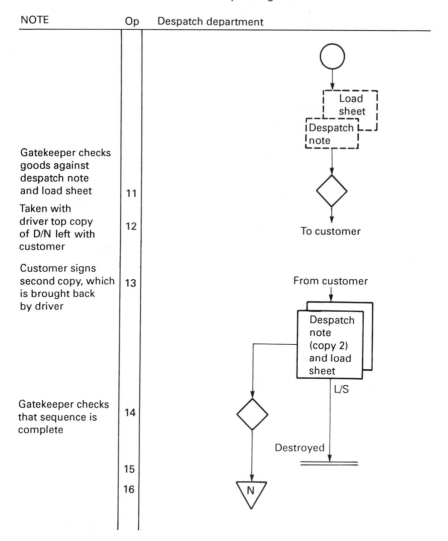

NOTE	Op	Despatch department
Gatekeeper checks goods against despatch note and load sheet	11	
Taken with driver top copy of D/N left with customer	12	To customer
Customer signs second copy, which is brought back by driver	13	From customer
Gatekeeper checks that sequence is complete	14	
	15	
	16	

[The following is an extract from the audit team's system notes.]

STOCK AVAILABILITY CHECK (Flowchart ref. 5)

1. STOCK AVAILABLE

On receipt of an order, the order details are checked for availability against the stock master file print-out and the order quantity deducted from the balance, to show the stock available (free stock). The sales order is marked with an 'A' to indicate availability.

2. STOCK UNAVAILABLE

The procedure is similar to that in 1 above. Items which are not available are marked 'R' (reorder) on the sales order and a letter is sent to the customer explaining that the goods are temporarily out of stock. A note is made on the order confirmation of the items not available.

2.6 Notes on the sales invoicing and sales ledger system

I discussed the sales invoicing and sales ledger system with the EDP manager and the assistant accountant. The system appears to operate as follows:

1. *Despatch notes are batched daily in the despatch department (see details in Document 2.5 above) and sent to EDP department. The data control clerk checks that the number of documents received agrees with the batch slip.*

2. *The clerk then enters individual despatch note details and batch totals into the mainframe computer. An edit program on the computer checks the batch total and the correctness of the account numbers used. (A check digit prevents invalid numbers from being accepted by the computer.) An error report is produced listing any input errors. These are then corrected by the control clerk and re-input and the error report is filed in date order.*

3. *The control clerk also inputs cash received sheets and journal adjustment sheets. These are prepared by the assistant accountant and are respectively a listing of cash received from customers and a listing of corrections to sales ledger accounts. Input of these is also checked via the error report.*

4. *After re-inputting as necessary, the clerk has produced a validated batch file. Every week this is run in the computer, together with the sales ledger master file, which lists customer details and balances, and the sales price master file. This run produces:*
   - *sales day book (weekly)*
   - *sales invoices (3 copies) (weekly)*
   - *statements for all customers (monthly)*
   - *an aged analysis of balances (monthly).*

The sales day book is compared with the totals of the despatch notes, cash received sheets and journals input to ensure that all have been completely entered. It is then filed in date order in the accounts department.

The sales invoices are returned to the sales dept., where they are matched with despatch notes filed there, to ensure that every invoice corresponds to a despatch note. The sales ledger clerk checks the accuracy of the casts and calculations of all invoices. One copy is then sent to the customer and the other 2 are filed, one copy in accounts dept. and one in the sales dept. with the despatch note.

One copy of the statement is sent to the customer. The other is filed in the accounts department.

The aged analysis of debtors shows, for each customer, the total balance outstanding and breaks it down into the amounts which are:
<30 days old
30−60 days old
60−90 days old
>90 days old.
The chief accountant reviews it every month and overdue items are followed up.

A sales ledger control account is maintained in the nominal ledger and is reconciled every month by the chief accountant to the list of balances on the aged analysis.

2.7 Extract from audit manager's review of the interim work

QUERY	REPLY
1. Is there any check to ensure that all despatch notes have resulted in an invoice, e.g. by a sequence check of despatch notes on file?	1. No, but they check from invoices to despatch notes.
2. Is there any check that the sales price master file is correct?	2. Yes. Every week, the sales dept. agree a print-out of the masterfile to a price list approved by the sales manager.
3. Is there any check that the aged analysis of debts is correct?	3. No.

2.8 Extract from audit programme, sales and debtors section

The following are key control objectives in ensuring that sales and debtors are correctly stated.
1. Customer orders require approval of credit and terms before acceptance.

2. Uncollectable amounts are promptly identified and provided for.
3. Goods despatched or services rendered are invoiced.
4. Invoices are for the correct amount.
5. Sales are recorded correctly as to account, amount and period.
6. Recorded invoices are for valid transactions.

QUESTIONS FOR DISCUSSION

Preliminary note: An important feature of any real-life sales system would be a system for ensuring that credits given to customers (for faulty goods, returns, etc.) are correctly authorized and recorded. For reasons of simplicity, the sales credit system has not been included in this case study.

1. Flowchart the system for taking and accepting orders.
2. For each of the control objectives stated in Document 2.8, identify what you consider to be the key controls or weaknesses in the system.
3. Based on your work in Question 2, suggest appropriate audit tests to ensure that the control objectives are met and that sales and debtors are correctly stated. Remember that your tests need not be exclusively systems tests: substantive testing and analytical review may also be required.

Relevant reading

Auditing Practices Committee (1989a):
    Auditing Guidelines: 2.204   Internal controls
                         4.407   Auditing in a computer environment
Woolf (1990), pp. 99−122, 439−507

Case 3
Green Fingers Limited

BACKGROUND

Green Fingers Ltd (GF) is a private company which specializes in planting and growing tomatoes and chrysanthemums. Its year-end is 31 October 19X1. Because of the company's small size, no interim audit is carried out. Instead, the audit work is performed during a single audit visit, which is to take place in December 19X1.

DOCUMENTS

3.1 Audit planning memorandum (extract)

ACTIVITIES

GF owns 7 acres of glasshouses. Two acres are planted with tomatoes, yielding on average 315 tons a year. The tomatoes are bought as seedlings and planted in mid-November each year. They produce two crops, in February and April. The remainder of the glasshouses are used for growing chrysanthemums: 450,000 bunches and 300,000 potted plants are grown annually; cultivation goes on throughout the year. GF employs 38 people.

CUSTOMERS

All the tomatoes are sold to Multiveg, a company which packs them and distributes them to supermarkets. All the cut flowers and 40% of the potted ones are sold via wholesale markets. The remaining 60% of potted flowers are sold to a large retail chain, Mega Stores plc.

PERSONNEL

The company's accounting function is the responsibility of the Managing Director, Mr Clayton, and 3 staff — the financial accountant and 2 clerks. Because of the small size of the department, it is difficult to achieve segregation of duties. Indeed, for efficiency, individual staff are required to deal with all aspects of transactions. Although the company is considering the purchase of a microcomputer, all records are currently kept manually.

Mr Clayton is closely involved in the day-to-day running of GF. His duties involve maintaining the fixed asset register, hiring all employees, authorizing all payments and reviewing all financial data. Mr Clayton is a qualified chartered accountant. The financial accountant, though experienced, is not qualified.

MATERIALITY LEVEL

This is determined in relation to GF's results as follows:

Item	Amount	%	Materiality estimate
	(£000)		
Turnover	800	0.5	£4,000
Shareholders' equity	182	2.5	£4,550
Current assets	110	1.0	£1,100
Total assets	400	0.5	£2,000

This gives a range of £1,100 to £4,550 as a possible range within which to establish a materiality level. In view of our previous satisfactory experience of this client, we have selected £4,000 as a materiality level.

3.2 Extract from permanent audit file

INDIVIDUALS PERFORMING KEY ACCOUNTING FUNCTIONS

List the names of key accounting personnel in the spaces provided. In the column below each name, indicate, using an 'X', the functions performed by that individual.

Name

Function	Mr Clayton Director	Mr Parsons Financial Accountant	Mr Scott Accounts Clerk	Miss Clarke Asst Accts Clerk	Auditors	Other
Nominal ledger			X			
Debtors' ledger			X			
Creditors' ledger				X		
Cashier		X				
Credit	X	X	(jointly)			
Despatch						X
Invoicing			X			
Purchasing	X					
Receiving						X
Payroll		X				
Cost accounting			N/A			
Personnel	X					
Income taxes					X	
Computer			N/A			
Other						

ACCOUNTING RECORDS KEPT

The key accounting records maintained are:

Nominal ledger
Sales ledger
Purchase ledger
Payroll clock cards
Payroll records
Fixed asset register
Sales day book
Purchase day book
Cash book

3.3   Extract from control information form

INSTRUCTIONS

This form is to be used to summarize the accounting systems and control procedures of a small business client. Place an 'X' in the appropriate column to indicate who performs each particular procedure. If a procedure is not applicable because of the nature of the client's business, enter 'N/A' in the column headed 'Not Done'.

This form is organized by audit components as follows:

Production or Service deals with:
• Purchases
• Creditors
• Stock
• Payroll
• Fixed assets

Sales deals with:
• Sales
• Debtors

Finance deals with:
• Bank and cash
• Loans
• Equity

Administration deals with:
• Taxation
• Commitments and contingencies

ACCOUNTING PROCEDURES
Production or Service

	Performed by				
	Owner/ Manager	*Bookkeeper/ Accountant*	*Asst Accounts Clerk*	*Other*	*Not Done*
1. (a) *Expenses incurred or purchases made above specified amount approved (Describe* ALL_____)	X				
(b) *A computerized detail of expenses exceeding specified amount is:*					
* System-generated_____					N/A
* Reviewed_____					N/A
* Compared to approved documents					N/A
2. *Goods checked and compared to packing slip or invoice before acceptance*			X		
3. (a) *Goods received note, purchase, order and invoice matched before purchase recorded*			X		
(b) *Goods received notes are initialled or otherwise cancelled after recording*			X		
4. *Record of returned goods matched to supplier credit notes*			X		

	Performed by				Not Done
	Owner/ Manager	Bookkeeper/ Accountant	Asst Accounts Clerk	Other	
5. Invoice additions, extensions and pricing checked			X		
6. Unmatched goods received notes and invoices investigated for inclusion in year-end accruals		X			
7. Nominal ledger account classification:					
(a) performed by			X		
(b) reviewed by		X			
8. (a) Suppliers' statements reconciled to the detail of creditors accounts DAILY *			X		
(b) Creditors' account balances reconciled to the control account MONTHLY *		X			
9. Expense reports reviewed					X
10. (a) Commissions approved					X
(b) Commissions reconciled to recorded sales ____					X
11. Other Detailed Analytical Review on a monthly basis on gross margins		X			
12. Personnel records maintained		X			
13. Approval of payroll:					
starters		X			
changes in rates of pay		X			
overtime pay		X			

leavers		X	
bonuses		X	
14. Time cards, time reports or piecework records approved		X	
15. Time paid reconciled to time worked *			X
16. Work paid reconciled to work produced (if pay is tied to production) *			X
17. Allocation of hours (indirect and direct) to activity or department reviewed or approved		X	X
18. Payments for sick leave and holidays approved	X		
19. Clerical accuracy of payroll checked	X		
20. Payroll reviewed for unusual amounts			
21. (a) Paypackets distributed		X	
(b) Cheques/bank transfers approved		X	
22. Other			
23. (a) Costs assigned to physical stock quantities		X	
(b) Costs reviewed			X
24. Actual costs compared with production cost budgets * —			X
25. Written instructions for stock counts prepared			X
26. Responsibility for taking physical stock		X	
27. Actual quantities are compared to perpetua' records YEARLY *			
28. Differences between physical counts and perpetual records investigated		X	

	Performed by				
	Owner/ Manager	*Bookkeeper/ Accountant*	*Asst Accounts Clerk*	*Other*	*Not Done*
29. Stock record adjustments approved	X				
30. Stock accounts adjusted for results of periodic physical counts *					X
31. Written stores requisition or despatch orders used for all issues of stock					X
32. Material leaving premises checked against goods despatch notes					X
33. Result of scrap gathering, measuring, recording, storing and disposal/recycling are reviewed *					X
34. Other					
35. (a) Stock levels and future use reviewed *DAILY* *	X				
(b) Comparisons of usage to quantities in stock are:					
Prepared/system-generated *					X
Reviewed *					X
36. Production and existing stock levels related to forecast of market and technological changes					X
37. Stock on hand is reviewed for 'old' items *		X			
38. Book value compared to net realizable value; adjustment recorded, if necessary *					X

39. Other _____		
40. Disposals authorized	X	
41. Gain or loss on sale recorded at the same time as related disposals	X	
42. Replaced assets and trade-ins written out of accounts at the same time as the related acquisition is recorded	X	
43. Fixed assets register maintained and reconciled to control accounts YEARLY	X	*
44. Adequacy of property insurance coverage reviewed ANNUALLY	X	*
45. Asset lives and depreciation methods for property additions set	X	
46. Schedules of written-down assets maintained	X	
47. Depreciation calculations checked for accuracy and overall reasonableness YEARLY	X	*
48. Other _____		

3.4 Extract from accounts for the year ended 31 October 19X0

GREEN FINGERS LIMITED

Profit and loss account for the year ended 31 October 19X0

	Note	19X0 £	19Y9 £
Turnover	2	800,823	701,781
Cost of sales		(789,325)	(731,144)
Gross profit (loss)		11,498	(29,363)
Distribution costs		(39,314)	(39,341)
Administrative expenses		(30,809)	(28,229)
Net operating loss	3	(58,625)	(96,933)
Other income	6	542	3,102
Interest payable	7	(10,362)	(5,423)
Loss before taxation		(68,445)	(99,254)
Taxation	8	3,114	26,500
Loss on ordinary activities after taxation		(65,331)	(72,754)
Dividends	9	–	–
Loss for the year		(65,331)	(72,754)
Statement of retained profits			
Balance at 1 November		202,592	275,346
Loss for the year		(65,331)	(72,754)
Balance at 31 October		137,261	202,592

GREEN FINGERS LIMITED

Balance sheet as at 31 October 19X0

	Note	19X0 £	19Y9 £
Fixed assets			
Tangible assets	10	275,879	297,960
Investments	11	13,905	13,905
		289,784	311,865

Current assets			
Stocks	12	56,324	58,697
Debtors	13	52,978	44,378
Cash at bank and in hand		1,306	48,138
		110,608	151,213
Creditors − amounts falling due within one year			
Trade and other creditors	14	99,692	97,804
Bank overdraft	16	10,898	−
Corporation tax		−	1,759
		110,590	99,563
Net current assets		18	51,650
Total assets less current liabilities		289,802	363,515
Creditors − amounts falling due after more than one year	17	60,000	61,413
Provision for liabilities and charges	18	−	3,114
Accruals and deferred income	19	47,648	51,503
Total assets less liabilities		182,154	247,485
Capital and reserves	20	20,150	20,150
Called-up share capital		24,743	24,743
Revaluation reserve		137,261	202,592
Profit and loss account			
		182,154	247,485

GREEN FINGERS LIMITED

Notes on the accounts − 31 October 19X0

1. *Accounting policies*
   (a) *Accounting convention*
       The accounts are prepared under the historical cost convention modified by the revaluation of certain fixed assets.

   (b) *Depreciation*
       Freehold land is not depreciated. The cost or valuation of other

fixed assets is written off over the expected useful lives of the assets as follows:

Freehold buildings	2% straight line
Glasshouses	5% straight line
Boiler installation − Buildings	2−5% straight line
− Machinery	5% straight line
Plant and equipment	15% reducing balance
Office fixtures and machinery	15% reducing balance
Motor vehicles	25% reducing balance
Aeroplane	20% reducing balance

(c) *Stocks and work in progress*
Stocks are valued at the lower of cost, on a first in, first out basis, and net realizable value after making due allowances for any obsolete and slow-moving items. The quantity of crops in the process of growing at the year-end is estimated by the directors. The valuation of this crop is at latest purchase price on a FIFO basis.

(d) *Deferred taxation*
Provision is made for deferred taxation, using the liability method, on short-term timing differences and all other material timing differences which are not expected to continue in the future.

(e) *Grants*
Horticultural grants are included in the balance sheet at the total received to date less the amounts credited to the profit and loss account, at the same rate as the relevant asset is depreciated.

(f) *Pension Benefits*
Pension benefits are funded over the employees' period of service. The company's contribution is charged to the profit and loss account as incurred.

2. *Turnover*
Turnover comprises the invoice value of goods and services supplied by the company exclusive of VAT, throughout the United Kingdom.

3. *Net operating loss* is stated after charging:	19X0	19Y9
	£	£
Depreciation of tangible fixed assets	28,832	30,230
Auditors' remuneration	2,500	2,200

4. *Staff costs*	19X0	19Y9
	£	£
Wages and salaries	244,566	234,026
Social security costs	22,040	20,026
Other pension costs	4,528	4,528
	271,134	258,580

This includes remuneration paid to directors of the company of £41,565 (19Y9−£49,065) − see Note 5.

5. *Emoluments of directors*	19X0	19Y9
	£	£
Fees	5,450	5,450
Remuneration, including pension		
contributions and benefits in kind	38,634	45,456
	44,084	50,906

6. *Other income*	19X0	19Y9
	£	£
Interest receivable	519	3,079
Rent	23	23
	542	3,102

7. *Interest payable*	19X0	19Y9
	£	£
Loans and overdrafts		
− repayable within 5 years	5,121	214
− repayable after 5 years	4,800	4,800
Hire-purchase interest	441	409
	10,362	5,423

8. *Taxation*	19X0	19Y9
	£	£
The credit based on the loss for the year comprises:		
Corporation tax	−	160
Deferred taxation:		
Accelerated capital allowances	(11,100)	(1,210)
Grants	1,633	1,226
Taxation losses	6,353	(26,676)
	(3,114)	(26,500)

9. *Dividends*
No dividend has been paid on the 4.2% cumulative preference shares since 31 October 19Y5. The arrears of dividend amount to £2,488.

10. *Tangible fixed assets*	At 1.11.Y9 £	Additions £	Disposals £	At 31.10.X0 £
Cost or valuation				
Freehold land and farms	17,118	–	–	17,118
Buildings	25,694	–	–	25,694
Glasshouses	141,807	–	–	141,807
Boiler installation				
– Buildings	13,134	–	–	13,134
– Machinery	170,281	–	–	170,281
Plant and equipment	216,072	6,751	–	222,823
Office fixtures and machinery	2,063	–	–	2,063
Motor vehicles	7,506	–	–	7,506
Aeroplane	11,704	–	–	11,704
	605,379	6,751	–	612,130
Depreciation				
Freehold land and farms	–	–	–	–
Buildings	3,598	514	–	4,112
Glasshouses	99,862	7,090	–	106,952
Boiler installation				
– Buildings	2,857	550	–	3,407
– Machinery	46,421	6,869	–	53,290
Plant and equipment	138,313	12,677	–	150,990
Office fixtures and machinery	1,831	34	–	1,865
Motor vehicles	4,252	814	–	5,066
Aeroplane	10,285	284	–	10,569
	307,419	28,832	–	336,251
Net book amounts	£297,960			£275,879

The freehold land, buildings, glasshouses and plant and equipment were revalued [ten years ago] at £105,403. Subsequent additions are stated at cost.

If they had not been revalued, freehold land, buildings, glasshouses and plant and equipment would have been carried in the balance sheet at 31 October 19X0 at:

	£
Cost	382,699
Accumulated depreciation	243,339
	139,360

The net book amount of plant and machinery for the company includes £4,026 (19Y9−£5,043) in respect of assets purchased under hire-purchase agreements.

11. *Fixed asset investments*

	Unlisted Investments
Cost at 31 October 19Y9 and 19X0	£13,905

The directors consider the value of unlisted investments to be not materially different from the value shown in the balance sheet.

A 10.74% shareholding is held in the ordinary shares of Year Round Flowers Limited.

12. *Stocks*

	19X0	19Y9
	£	£
Cuttings and seeds	21,549	23,992
Fuel and oils	10,283	16,892
Packing materials	6,135	7,107
Fertilizers and insecticides	3,449	3,558
Other	14,908	7,148
	56,324	58,697

The directors consider the replacement cost of stocks to be not materially different from the value shown in the balance sheet.

13. *Debtors*

	19X0	19Y9
	£	£
Due within one year:		
Trade debtors	40,905	33,222
Other debtors	2,420	5,875
Prepayments and accrued income	9,653	5,281
	52,978	44,378

14. *Trade and other creditors*

	19X0	19Y9
	£	£
Trade creditors	51,315	54,444
Other creditors	18,052	12,407

Other taxation and social security	15,098	13,848
Obligations under finance leases (Note 15)	1,413	2,406
Accruals and deferred income	13,814	14,699
	99,692	97,804

15. *Obligations under finance leases*
The capital amounts due under finance lease obligations are as follows:

	19X0	19Y9
	£	£
Within one year	1,413	2,406
Within two to five years	–	1,413
	1,413	3,819

16. *Bank overdraft*
The company has given a legal mortgage on the freehold land and buildings and a floating charge on all other property in respect of any bank overdrafts.

17. *Creditors* – amounts falling due after more than one year

	19X0	19Y9
	£	£
Term loan	60,000	60,000
Obligations under finance leases (Note 15)	–	1,413
	60,000	61,413

The loan is secured by fixed and floating charges over all the assets of the company, ranking pari passu with the similar charges in favour of the company's bankers (Note 16).

The loan is repayable by way of eight half-yearly instalments of £7,500 commencing June 19X2.

The interest rate payable in respect of the loan is 8% per annum.

18. *Provision for liabilities and charges*

Deferred taxation – potential and provided:	19X0	19Y9
	£	£
Accelerated capital allowances	64,806	75,906
Grants	(13,818)	(15,451)
Taxation losses	(50,988)	(57,341)
	–	3,114

19. *Accruals and deferred income*	19X0	19Y9
	£	£
Balance at 1 November 19Y9	51,503	55,589
Grants received in the year	–	–
Credited to profit and loss	(3,855)	(4,086)
Balance at 31 October 19X0	47,648	51,503

20. *Called-up share capital*	19X0	19Y9
	£	£
Authorized:		
25,000 shares of £1 each	25,000	25,000
Allotted and fully paid:		
7,850 'A' ordinary shares of £1 each	7,850	7,850
450 'B' ordinary shares of £1 each	450	450
	8,300	8,300
11,850 4.2% cumulative preference shares of £1 each	11,850	11,850
	20,150	20,150

21. *Employees*

The average number of employees during the year was 38 (19Y9−38) involved in various aspects of the company's trade.

22. *Commitments*

Capital commitments − authorized future capital expenditure for which contracts have been awarded amounts to £32,039 (19Y9 − nil).

GREEN FINGERS LIMITED

Trading account: year ended 31 October 19X0

	Statement	19X0 £	19Y9 £
Sales		800,823	701,781
Cost of sales			
Wages and national insurance contributions		205,901	189,170
Fuel		168,187	137,304
Fertilizers and insecticides		28,310	26,505
Cuttings and seeds		116,201	115,399
Discount received		(7,235)	(5,178)

		30,690	26,053
Production consumables		30,690	26,053
Produce for resale		10,767	11,419
Commission and charges		73,794	69,615
Farm cost of sales		5,835	5,807
		632,450	576,094
Gross margin		168,373	125,687
Direct expenses	I	156,875	155,050
Gross profit (loss)		11,498	(29,363)
Overheads			
Distribution costs	II	(39,314)	(39,341)
Administrative expenses	III	(30,809)	(28,229)
Net operating loss		(58,625)	(96,933)

Statement I: Direct expenses	19X0	19Y9
	£	£
Repairs and renewals	12,347	15,365
Motor vehicle expenses	16,216	14,710
Vehicle leasing	96	96
Boxes and packing materials	32,996	27,886
Travelling expenses	4,773	3,471
Insurance	11,203	9,329
Telephone	3,776	3,072
Postage	315	341
Printing and stationery	727	607
Rates	1,292	1,119
Water charges	1,372	1,036
Sundry expenses	1,336	1,185
Depreciation		
Glasshouse	7,090	7,090
Boiler installation	7,419	7,420
Buildings	514	514
Plant and equipment	12,677	13,722
Motor vehicles	814	1,087
Aeroplane	284	355
Horticultural grants	(3,855)	(4,086)
Profit on disposal of fixed assets	–	(12)
Directors' remuneration:		
Salaries	32,500	40,000
Employers' national insurance	3,918	1,678

Fees	5,450	5,450
Pensions	3,615	3,615
	156,875	155,050

Statement II: Distribution Costs	19X0	19Y9
Carriage	£39,314	£39,341

Statement III: Administrative expenses	19X0	19Y9
	£	£
Administrative salaries	19,750	18,667
Subscription	735	694
Legal and professional fees	5,540	4,488
Bank charges	850	838
Audit and accountancy	3,900	3,500
Depreciation:		
Office fixtures and fittings	34	42
	30,809	28,229

3.5 Production or Service: control objectives

Purchases and creditors
1. Expenditure on goods or services is made only with proper authorization.
2. Goods, services, expenses, fixed assets and related liabilities are recorded correctly as to account, amount and period.

Payroll
3. Salaries, wages and related costs are incurred only for work authorized and performed.
4. Salaries, wages and related costs are calculated at the proper rate.
5. Salaries, wages, related costs and liabilities are recorded correctly as to account, amount and period.

Stocks and work in progress
6. Costs are assigned to stock and work in progress at year-end in accordance with the stated valuation method.
7. Stock and work in progress quantities are accurately recorded and extended.
8. Physical loss of stock is prevented or promptly detected.
9. Obsolete, slow-moving and excess stock is prevented or promptly detected and provided for.
10. Stock and work in progress are carried at the lower of cost and net realizable value.

Property, plant and equipment

11. Disposal and scrapping of plant are identified and recorded correctly as to account, amount and period.
12. Physical loss of property, plant and equipment is prevented.
13. Depreciation is calculated using proper lives and methods.

3.6   Extracts from an interview with Mr Clayton

Alan Andrews (A), the audit senior, interviewed Mr Clayton (C) on 14 October to discuss various matters which were relevant to the audit.

A   Can we talk about the stock system you have here, Mr Clayton?

C   Yes, sure. We keep − that is, the accountant keeps − a set of cards which he enters up with all the movements in and out. We have a separate card for every different type of stock item. When we do a stocktake, we compare the stock records with the cards and I authorize any adjustments that need to be put through.

A   Is that the year-end stocktake?

C   Yes. We do one count, on 31 October.

A   How is that organized?

C   The nursery manager and a couple of the staff do the counts of packing materials, chemicals and fuel. They record their results on stock-sheets which the accountant prices up. I'm responsible for estimating the quantity of growing crops.

A   How do you do that?

C   I work to a rule of thumb about the number of plants to an acre, and I adjust it if necessary, say for areas that have been a bit in the shade and produced a thinner crop. It's not perfect, but it's fairly accurate. We don't tend to get any major surprises when we work out the final figure.

A   I see. And then how do you value stock?

C   We use a FIFO basis for everything. For chemicals and so on, we just refer to the stock cards, which show the invoice price for every delivery, and base our valuation on that. When we value growing crops, we base the valuation on the latest purchase price of all the items used in the cultivation process.

A   What about cut flowers and tomatoes?

C   Those are despatched as soon as they're harvested, so we don't have any in stock.

A I don't suppose you have any problems with obsolescence.

C Not really, given the nature of this business. The only worry we have that way is crop failure. So far, we've been lucky, but there's a virus in the UK at the moment called thripps, which could have a dire effect on the flower crop. We do all we can to keep that kind of thing at bay, but the risk is still there.

A To change the subject a bit; what are your main expenses?

C Two things − wages and fuel. The other expenses are less important.

A Have they varied much over recent years?

C Wages are fixed by a wages board. There was a 9% pay increase in January this year. Otherwise, there's been nothing to affect the wage level. Employee numbers haven't changed since last year. We have a very stable workforce. Unfortunately, the fuel price has moved about a lot. We can use coal or oil to heat the glasshouses − we have two boilers − and we switch periodically to whichever is cheaper to run. At the moment, it's oil. In fact, we've bought oil forward. We hope we have enough to see us through the coming winter ...

QUESTIONS FOR DISCUSSION

1. What are the particular features of a small company, such as GF, which create problems for the auditor?
2. For the Production or Service control objectives listed in Document 3.5:
   (a) identify the key controls which exist in GF's system;
   (b) suggest audit tests (including systems tests, analytical review and substantive tests) which will ensure that the control objectives are being achieved.

Relevant reading

Auditing Practices Committee (1989b)
ICAEW (1979)
Woolf (1990), pp. 297−305

Case 4
Esparto Limited

BACKGROUND

Esparto Ltd (E) is a paper and cardboard manufacturing company whose year-end is 31 March 1989. The auditors are visiting the company early in January 1989 in order to plan their audit approach for the 1989 year-end. They have obtained copies of the 1989 management accounts and are comparing these with budgets and actual results for previous years in order to gain an insight into E's performance and to identify any areas which may pose problems at the year-end.

DOCUMENTS

4.1 Esparto Limited: Summarized management accounts Esparto Limited management accounts: balance sheets

| | Actual | | | Budget | Actual movement | |
| | | | | | 9M 89/12M 88 | |
	12M 31.3.87 £000	12M 31.3.88 £000	9M 31.12.88 £000	9M 31.12.88 £000	£000	%
Fixed assets	940	1,156	1,200	1,205	44	3.81
Current assets						
Stocks	407	441	280	320	−161	−36.50
Debtors	415	454	474	477	20	4.40
Due from subsidiaries	30	–	30	50	30	100.00
Bank and cash	101	–	–	6	–	–
	953	895	784	853	−111	−12.40
Current liabilities						
Bank overdraft	–	29	30	–	1	3.45
Obligations under finance leases	222	230	207	210	−23	−10.00
Creditors	350	380	296	330	−84	−22.10
Taxation	102	82	84	86	2	2.44
Proposed dividends	20	30	–	30	−30	−100.00
	694	751	617	656	−134	−17.84
Net current assets	259	144	167	197	23	15.97
Total net assets	1,199	1,300	1,367	1,402	67	5.15

Financed by:

Share capital	500	500	500	500	–	0.00
Reserves	639	740	807	842	67	9.05
Revaluation reserves	60	60	60	60	–	0.00
Total capital and reserves	1,199	1,300	1,367	1,402	67	5.15

Esparto Limited management accounts: profit and loss accounts

	Actual			Budget		Movement	
	12M	12M	9M	9M	12M	Bud. 89/Act. 88	
	31.3.87	31.3.88	31.12.88	31.12.88	31.3.89		
	£000	£000	£000	£000	£000	£000	%
Sales	3,769	3,949	2,952	3,115	4,153	204	5.17
Less: Direct materials	1,409	1,539	1,204	1,160	1,547	8	0.52
Direct labour	400	428	332	335	446	18	4.20
	1,960	1,982	1,416	1,620	2,160	178	8.98
Overheads	723	770	615	625	833	63	8.18
Gross profit	1,237	1,212	801	995	1,327	115	9.49

	12M 31.3.87	12M 31.3.88	9M 31.12.88	9M 31.12.88	12M 31.3.89	66	11.72
...ing and admin expenses	624	563	348	472	629	66	11.72
General expenses	425	432	350	321	429	-3	-0.69
Profit before tax	188	217	103	202	269	52	23.96
Taxation	85	86	36	70	93	7	8.14
Profit after tax	103	131	67	132	176	45	34.35
Dividends	20	30	-	30	40	10	33.33
Retained profit	83	101	67	102	136	35	34.65

Esparto Limited management accounts: overheads and expenses

	Actual			Budget		Movement	
						Bud. 89/Act. 88	
	12M 31.3.87 £000	12M 31.3.88 £000	9M 31.12.88 £000	9M 31.12.88 £000	12M 31.3.89 £000	£000	%
Overheads							
Indirect labour	85	89	72	72	96	7	7.87
Rent	360	380	299	300	400	20	5.26
Rates	50	60	51	55	73	13	21.67
Power and light	80	70	58	52	69	-1	-1.43
Maintenance	65	22	22	36	48	26	118.18
Depreciation	59	81	63	64	85	4	4.94
Consumables	24	20	16	14	19	-1	-5.00
Finance charges	-	48	34	32	43	-5	-10.42
Total	723	770	615	625	833	63	8.18

General expenses							
Salaries	275	290	228	224	299	9	3.10
Office rent and rates	50	65	51	50	67	2	3.08
Telephone	3	5	3	2	3	−2	−40.00
Insurance	12	15	12	10	13	−2	−13.33
Bad debt provision	4	2	–	2	3	1	50.00
Audit	10	12	9	8	11	−1	−8.33
Sundries	2	1	1	1	1	–	0.00
Legal	17	15	13	7	9	−6	−40.00
Management charges	32	20	18	12	16	−4	−20.00
Repairs and renewals	20	7	15	5	7	–	0.00
Total	425	432	350	321	429	−3	−0.69
Selling expenses							
Salaries	70	74	37	36	48	−26	−35.14
Commission	30	32	25	30	40	8	25.00
Advertising and marketing	254	165	72	186	248	83	50.30
Travel and entertainment	55	62	33	40	53	−9	−14.52
Carriage	215	230	181	180	240	10	4.35
Total	624	563	348	472	629	66	11.72

4.2   Extract from permanent audit file

The following schedule summarizes key ratios for Esparto Ltd since the year ended 31 March 1987.

	Actual			*Budget*
Key ratios	*12M*	*12M*	*9M*	*9M*
	31.3.87	*31.3.88*	*31.12.88*	*31.12.88*
Asset turnover	*3.14*	*3.04*	*2.16*	*2.22*
Debtors turnover	*9.08*	*8.70*	*6.23*	*6.53*
Average collection period	*40.19*	*41.96*	*43.99*	*41.96*
Average payment period	*90.67*	*90.12*	*67.36*	*77.95*
Current ratio	*1.37*	*1.19*	*1.27*	*1.30*
Quick ratio	*0.79*	*0.60*	*0.82*	*0.81*
ROCE	*0.16*	*0.17*	*0.08*	*0.14*

4.3   Extract from audit planning memorandum

GROUP STRUCTURE AND POLICY

Esparto Ltd is a wholly owned subsidiary of Parchment plc, a London-based multinational group. E's factory and offices are located in Worksop. E has a number of fellow subsidiaries in the UK. Parchment has adopted a policy in recent years of encouraging decentralization and local autonomy, so that decision-making is increasingly delegated to local management. Expenditure controlled at local level includes capital investment (up to a limit of £200,000) and all routine overheads, including marketing and advertising.

All dividends declared by Parchment subsidiaries are passed up to group headquarters. Parchment imposes a management charge on its subsidiaries to reflect their share of the services provided for them by the group, such as their use of group accounting and computing services. The management charge is determined centrally and is outside the control of individual subsidiaries. VAT is charged on the management charge.

ACTIVITIES

E produces different types of cardboard. It manufactures cardboard sheets, which it sells to fellow subsidiaries, and high quality corrugated cartons which it supplies to the whisky, chemical, electrical and food sectors. Its main raw material is paper, which it purchases directly from Sweden, paying for it in dollars. Different grades of paper are used, depending on the type of cardboard to be manufactured. It takes 6 weeks for E to receive an order from Sweden once it has been placed.

4.4   Extract from interview with David Weeks

Present: Jean Bailey (B), Audit Manager
            David Weeks (W), Managing Director of Esparto

B   Could you tell me what Esparto's sales targets are for the future?

W   Our aim is to achieve a steady 5% annual growth in sales while keeping
      gross contribution at about 52%.

B   And what action is the company taking to achieve this?

W   We're doing a number of things. Obviously, marketing is crucial. Our
      spending in that area has dropped over the last couple of years, but
      we intend to increase it significantly. We plan a big campaign in the
      relevant trade publications, and we shall be attending trade fairs and
      exhibitions in the UK and abroad. The quality of what we sell is very
      important too. We put a lot of stress on quality control, and we're
      steadily upgrading our fixed assets. Over the past 2 years, we've brought
      in new stitchers and glue units and made a number of improvements
      to the corrugating machine.

B   Is this a competitive market?

W   This is an extremely competitive market. There is substantial over-capacity
      at the moment, and the reaction in the industry is to cut prices and make
      special promotional offers. We have to push particularly hard for sales at
      the moment because we lost a major customer recently. It was Carton
      & Case, who were taken over by a competitor of ours, Containers plc.
      Naturally, Containers has got all their business, and we have to compensate
      for that . . .

4.5   Extract from permanent audit file

BUDGET SYSTEM
E's budgeting system is largely dictated by the requirements of the Parchment
group. The budgeting process begins in November each year, when divisional
heads within E are required to submit outline budgets for their divisions.
Particular stress is laid on the preparation of capital budgets for plant and
equipment.

The management accountant, in conjunction with E's finance director,
uses this information to prepare a budget for the company as a whole, which
covers the 12 months from 1 April to 31 March. This company-wide budget
is then discussed with the management team at Parchment, and simultaneously with divisional heads at E until a final budget has been agreed. This
is then broken down again into divisional budgets and these are phased into
monthly budgets.

Divisional results against budget are reported to, and monitored by, E's management accountant and financial director. E's overall results are reported to Parchment, together with an explanation of major variations from budget.

There is only limited scope for Parchment's subsidiaries to revise their budgets after 1 April each year. Revision would be permitted in case of a major upheaval, such as the closure or complete reorganization of a plant, but 'fine-tuning' the budget does not occur.

QUESTIONS FOR DISCUSSION

1. You are responsible for planning the audit of Esparto for the year ending 31 March 1988. Using the information the case study gives about the company, identify those areas which you consider to present potential audit risks.
2. Using the schedules summarizing management accounts, identify the main trends in the company's performance this year. What questions should the auditor ask in order to gain a fuller understanding of E's performance and prospects?

Relevant reading

Auditing Practices Committee (1989a):
  Auditing Guidelines: 4.417 Analytical review
Coopers & Lybrand (1985), pp. 210–13
Woolf (1990), pp. 240–9

Case 5
The Enormous Electrical Company

BACKGROUND

The Enormous Electrical Company Ltd (EE) was formed in March 19X8 by the merger of two smaller companies. It retails household electrical appliances of all kinds through a chain of thirty shops which it owns all over the UK. These are supplied from three warehouses, in Bristol, Birmingham and Glasgow. EE's first financial statements are for the period ending 31 December 19X8. The newly appointed financial controller drafted the stocktaking instructions to be followed by the warehouse and shop managers. The warehouse instructions are given in Document 5.1. EE's auditors attended all the three warehouse stocktakes (and a sample of the counts at shops). The audit working papers for the Bristol warehouse are given in Document 5.2.

DOCUMENTS

5.1   The Enormous Electrical Co. Ltd − Internal memo

FROM   James Wilson, Financial Controller   4 November 19X8
TO   Peter Drake, Bristol warehouse
        Frank Moore, Birmingham warehouse
        Bill Drew, Glasgow warehouse

STOCKTAKING INSTRUCTIONS

1.   The company's financial year-end will be 31 December 19X8 and a full count is to be carried out of all stocks held in the warehouses at that date. Please read the following instructions carefully and ensure that they are adhered to. Contact me as soon as possible if you need any clarification or if you anticipate any problems.

2.   PREPARATION
The warehouse is to be tidied thoroughly in the week before the stocktake. Packing cases should be stacked as closely as possible, to allow staff to move freely. The warehouse is to be divided into clearly defined areas. Each area will be assigned to one of the warehouse staff, who will be responsible for counting the stock contained in it. The warehouse manager will be responsible for circulating these instructions to staff, dealing with any queries and ensuring that final stocksheets are sent to HO. It is also the responsibility of managers to identify obsolete or damaged stock.

3. COUNTING PROCEDURES

A sample stocksheet is shown in Appendix A to this memo. A supply of photocopies of this sheet is to be taken, for issue to staff. Staff should return completed sheets promptly to the warehouse manager. Each item of stock (case, box, etc.) should be marked with chalk when it has been counted. After completing the count, the person responsible should inspect the area to ensure that there are no unmarked items. Goods will have to be removed from the warehouse during 30 and 31 December, as they must reach shops in time for our January sale. As far as possible, counters should complete counting in their areas before allowing the movement of goods.

4. FOLLOW-UP

When all rough stocksheets have been returned, managers should review them and enquire into the reasons for any unexpectedly high or low stock figures. When this has been done, the rough sheets should be transcribed on to final sheets by a member of the clerical staff, to ensure that they are legible. The final sheets should then be returned to HO. Managers should make a note of the first goods inward and goods outward note numbers raised on 1 January 19X9 and send this information to HO for cut-off purposes.

Thank you in advance for your co-operation.

James

APPENDIX A

SPECIMEN STOCK SHEET

LOCATION

NAME OF STOCKTAKER

STOCK CODE   QUANTITY   UNIT*

* Specify boxes, dozen, each, etc.

5.2　Notes on attendance at the Enormous Electrical Co.'s stocktake at Bristol on 31 December 19X8

I attended EE's stocktake at its warehouse on the Excelsior Industrial Estate between 9.30 a.m. and 5.30 p.m. on 31 December. During this time, I discussed the stocktaking procedures with the warehouse manager, Mr Drake, and toured the warehouse to observe the stocktake. The warehouse was tidy and the count appeared to be going on in an orderly fashion, with items being marked off as they were counted. I performed the following test counts:

(a) From stock sheets to physical stock:

STOCK CODE	NOTES	QTY PER SHEET	QTY COUNTED
AJ123		12	12
M3000	(1)	6	5+1
F234		19	19
AS19		100	100
EM236		63	63
BII32		231	231
DE470	(2)	85	50
SR288		12	12
EM670		11	11
FH678		76	76
AK427		100	100
Q345	(3)	54	45
M2500		23	23
DJ688	(4)	16	13
SDD358		9	9

(b) From physical stock to stocksheets

STOCK CODE	NOTES	QTY COUNTED	QTY PER SHEET
QWE112		37	37
F1000		68	68
ET667	(5)	130	120
WSC987	(6)	335	339
EM457		34	34
W2790		32	32
DJ3456		23	23
DE379		8	8
DJ4326	(6)	97	100

Q3098		35	35
DF4563		98	98
JUS333		12	12
SD4578	(6)	500	510
FR8748		97	97
ED5544		18	18

NOTES:

(1) *The difference on this line — Hotpoint washing machines — arose because I originally omitted the one damaged machine which had been moved to a separate part of the warehouse.*

(2) *35 of this item had been removed from the warehouse for distribution to shops between the time they were counted and the time I carried out my test.*

(3) *9 of this item had been removed for distribution before I could count them.*

(4) *Presumably the same reason for the difference as in (2) and (3) above.*

(5) *This difference arose because I mistakenly counted 10 of item EX661 as ET667.*

(6) *I was unable to discuss these differences with the storeman responsible, as he had finished for the day and gone home. They seem to have been simple mistakes. However, since the items involved are relatively low-value ones — electric kettles, blankets and toasters — and the numbers involved are so large, the error cannot be described as material and does not require further investigation.*

Conclusion: On the basis of the work done and the explanations I have received, I conclude that the stocktake has been correctly carried out and the stock quantities notified to HO are materially correct.

QUESTIONS FOR DISCUSSION

1. What controls are present in the stocktaking instructions issued to the warehouse managers? What controls have been omitted and what effect might this omission have on the results of the stocktake?

2. In your opinion, is there any other audit work which should have been carried out at this stocktake? What would it have achieved? Do you consider that the auditor has drawn the right conclusions from his findings?

Relevant reading

Auditing Practices Committee (1989a):
   Auditing Guidelines: 4.405   Attendance at stocktaking
Woolf (1990), pp. 223−40

Case 6
Technical Wizardry Limited

BACKGROUND

Technical Wizardry Ltd (TW) was originally set up in 1937 as the Typewriter Wholesaling Co. Ltd. The change of name reflects its strategy of moving into a new market in response to the decline in demand for typewriters and the increasing use of word processors and microcomputers in business. TW continues to sell typewriters but has gradually moved into the computer market, beginning by selling computer printers and going on to develop two computers of its own: the T700 and T35.

TW's year-end is 31 December and this case takes place in mid-January 19X1, during the latter part of the 19X0 audit. TW's profit before tax for 19X0 is expected to be about £15,000 on a turnover of £3 million. The auditors have completed the systems work and stocktaking attendance, with satisfactory results, and are now considering what tests need to be performed on stock valuation. Extracts from their working papers are given below.

DOCUMENTS

6.1 TW Ltd: stock summary

	19X0 £000	19Y9 £000
Typewriters	30	75
Printers	175	100
Typewriter spares	95	120
Printer spares	100	80
T700 computers	500	450
T35 computers:		
completed	50	–
work in progress	150	–
TOTAL	1,100	825

NB the 19X0 figures are subject to audit.

6.2 Extract from stock systems notes

Typewriter, printer and spares stock records are held on a microcomputer. Each different stock item is defined by a unique numerical code. Details of receipts of goods from suppliers and despatches to customers are input daily. The system can hold records of stock at 3 different purchase prices — current price and the 2 previous prices. It is rare for prices to change more often than twice a year. A number of reports can be produced by the computer, including:

Report no.	Frequency	Contents
001	Weekly	Receipts into stores analysed by stock code no.
002	Weekly	Issues from stores analysed by stock code no.
003	On demand	Movements over past 6 months of any stock item
004	Monthly	Aged analysis of stock by stock code no. and in total
005	Monthly	Stock items without any movement during the month
006	On demand	Current purchase price and previous price(s) over past 6 months of any stock item

The records for the stocks of T700 and T35 computers are kept manually on cards. The cards show the following information for each stock movement:

Date of receipt or issue
Quantity received/issued
Serial no of TW's goods received note/despatch note
Balance in stock

6.3 004 report totals at 31 December 19X0

```
TOTALS OF 004 REPORTS AS AT 31.12.X0
TYPEWRITERS                                    £
TOTAL STOCK                                30174
< 1 MONTH OLD                               9756
1-2 MONTHS OLD                             11234
2-3 MONTHS OLD                              8756
3-4 MONTHS OLD                               428
```

4–5 MONTHS OLD	NIL
5–6 MONTHS OLD	NIL
6–12 MONTHS OLD	NIL
> 12 MONTHS OLD	NIL

PRINTERS

TOTAL	174876
< 1 MONTH OLD	65756
1–2 MONTHS OLD	87432
2–3 MONTHS OLD	18904
3–4 MONTHS OLD	2784
4–5 MONTHS OLD	NIL
5–6 MONTHS OLD	NIL
6–12 MONTHS OLD	NIL
>12 MONTHS OLD	NIL

TYPEWRITERSPARES

TOTAL	95023
< 1 MONTH OLD	1500
1–2 MONTHS OLD	34211
2–3 MONTHS OLD	15678
3–4 MONTHS OLD	10877
4–5 MONTHS OLD	NIL
5–6 MONTHS OLD	4566
6–12 MONTHS OLD	18888
> 12 MONTHS OLD	9303

PRINTER SPARES

TOTAL	99566
< 1 MONTH OLD	45557
1–2 MONTHS OLD	27644
2–3 MONTHS OLD	13428
3–4 MONTHS OLD	7685
4–5 MONTHS OLD	3344
5–6 MONTHS OLD	1908
6–12 MONTHS OLD	NIL
> 12 MONTHS OLD	NIL

6.4 File note on T700s

T700s are manufactured for TW in Ruritania by a subcontractor. TW imports them, carries out a quality control check in its warehouse and test centre near Heathrow and then repackages the computers. Because Ruritanian wage levels are low, this is much cheaper than making the

T700 here in the UK. TW had some quality problems in the early years of this arrangement, but standards have improved as the Ruritanians gained experience and installed effective inspection procedures of their own. Returns last year were less than 0.25% of sales.

TW pays for the computers in Ruritanian drachmas (RDR). The price throughout 19X0 has been 6,000 RDR. In previous years, TW has bought RDR forward in order to reduce its exposure to exchange movements, but this year, for the first time it has bought spot, as a result of the finance director's theory that the RDR was overvalued and likely to fall heavily against the £. The average rate for the last 4 months of 19X0 has been:

Sept.	6.0 RDR = £1
Oct.	5.5 RDR = £1
Nov.	6.5 RDR = £1
Dec.	7.5 RDR = £1

Costs of handling, quality control and repackaging at the Heathrow site are estimated at £19 per machine, and this is added to the purchase price in the stock valuation.

At 31 December TW has 500 T700s in stock, all bought from Ruritania in the last 4 months. It has valued them at average cost. The finance director has calculated an average exchange rate based on the 4 month-end rates: 6.375 RDR = £1.

6.5 Extract from TW's price list effective from 1 January 19X1

	Gross £	VAT £	Net £
T700	1,725	225	1,500
T35	3,450	450	3,000

(NB: Discounts are available on bulk orders of T35s, starting at 7.5% for orders of 6. Ask your TW rep for further details.)

6.6 Audit file note on T35s

The T35 is a laptop microcomputer aimed in particular at sales representatives and others who need a small, easily portable computer. TW introduced it just over a year ago. Until August this year, T35s were manufactured for TW in Utopia on the same basis as the T700 in Ruritania. TW gradually became dissatisfied with the quality of the imports and took the decision to start production in the UK. A small electronics company, Chips With Everything Ltd, was acquired as a

TW *subsidiary in May and began full-scale production of the computer in August.*

There have been numerous production problems in the UK, because of the inexperience of the workforce and defects in components supplied. As a result, none of the T35s made in the UK has been sold. The finished goods stock represents the last of the Utopian production, mostly bought in October 19X0 and valued at a purchase price of £2,500 each. (Imported T35s were paid for in £ sterling.)

The work in progress (WIP) is all UK production and can be analysed as:

	£000
25% complete	20
50% complete	70
Held back for rectification	60
	150

WIP has been valued on the basis of its stage of completion. Costs accrue evenly over the production process. Finished cost of the UK-produced computers is £2,850 each.

The computers requiring rectification were completed in November. Inspection revealed that they suffer from a major fault which will require the disk drive to be removed and replaced at an estimated additional cost of approx £250 each. Replacement work will be carried out in January 19X1.

QUESTIONS FOR DISCUSSION

1. What problem areas do you see with regard to the valuation of TW's stock?
2. Assuming that systems testing and stocktaking attendance have had satisfactory results, what audit tests should now be performed to ensure that the stock valuation is correct or to identify any possible misstatement?

Relevant reading

Auditing Practices Committee (1989a)
ICAEW Statements on Auditing and Reporting:
  5.903 Stock-in-trade and work in progress
Woolf (1990), pp. 223–40
Coopers & Lybrand (1985), pp. 310–14

Case 7
Warehousemasters Limited

BACKGROUND

Warehousemasters Ltd (W) specializes in the design, manufacture and installation of tailor-made storage equipment. Its products and services range from a few yards of shelving to the design and installation of major warehouses.

Until recently, all W's sales were in the UK, but in the financial year just ended it undertook a major export drive in an attempt to improve its declining sales. This was successful and it now has customers in the USA and Italy.

W's auditors have as usual performed an interim audit visit to the company in August 19X7. The company's year-end (30 September) falls in their busy season and they try to perform as many tests as possible at the interim stage to save time later on. Mike Small, the senior in charge of the audit, is reviewing the interim tests with the aim of deciding what work should be done at the final audit, which is scheduled to start on 10 October. Work must be completed and the audit report signed by 31 October.

DOCUMENTS

7.1 Warehousemasters Ltd: Extracts from permanent audit file; sales systems notes

SALES OF GOODS
On despatch of the goods from the warehouse a multi-part despatch note is raised:
Copy 1 goes with goods to customer
Copy 2 is retained in stores dept to update records of stock levels
Copy 3 is sent to sales invoicing dept, used as basis for invoice and then filed with a copy invoice.
Despatch notes are sequentially numbered. Every period-end a check is performed to ensure that all despatch note numbers are accounted for, and any missing ones are followed up.

SALES OF SERVICES (design, consultancy etc.)
The computerized time accounting system records the costs of staff time. This is used as a basis for invoicing and a copy of the relevant print-out is filed with the sales invoice. Contracts are given sequential job numbers, and a sequence check is made periodically to ensure all have been invoiced on completion.

SALES LEDGER

This is interfaced with the sales invoicing system so that as invoices are raised they are automatically posted to the ledger.

A print-out of the ledger is run every period-end giving details of every account.

The layout of an account is typically as follows:

0003456 BLOGGINS LTD (CREDIT LIMIT £4000)

	CR	DR
1.3.X7 OPENING BAL	2345.00	
11.3.X7 INV NO 2347	1267.00	
23.3.X7 CASH		345.00
23.3.X7 CREDIT NOTE NO 126		500.00
31.3.X7 CLOSING BAL		2767.00
	----------	----------
	3612.00	3612.00
	----------	----------

Each customer is sent a monthly statement which is a duplicate of the sales ledger account.

AGED DEBTORS LISTING

This is printed every month and shows the balance on each account broken down by the age of the unpaid invoices:

ACC NO	TOTAL	CURRENT MONTH	0–30 DAYS	30–60 DAYS	60–90 DAYS	>90 DAYS
	£	£	£	£	£	£
0003456	2767	1267	NIL	790	310	400

CREDIT CONTROL

New customers are required to produce 2 references — from a bank and a current supplier — before they are allowed credit. The amount allowed is decided by the credit controller.

The controller reviews the monthly aged listing and telephones customers whose balances include items more than 60 days old.

After items are > 90 days old, a reminder letter is sent, with a sterner letter 14 days later. 3 weeks thereafter, a late payer will receive a solicitor's letter and may eventually be sued.

7.2 Extracts from interim audit working papers (sales section)

Test 1

OBJECTIVE
To ensure that all invoices
(a) represent despatches of goods/provision of services;
(b) are arithmetically correct.

WORK DONE
Selected a representative sample of 25 invoices for goods and 25 for services.
(a) Traced details of goods via copy despatch notes to stock issue records, and traced services details to time sheet summary record maintained by Design and Consultancy Department.
(b) Checked additions and calculations on each invoice.
See attached for details. [NB: Not included in case study.]

RESULTS
No errors were found.

CONCLUSION
All invoices relate to provision of goods/services and are arithmetically correct.

Test 2

OBJECTIVE
To ensure that all invoices are correctly posted to the sales ledger.

WORK DONE
Selected a representative sample of 30 sales invoices and ensured that they had been posted to the correct customer's sales ledger account in the correct period.
* See attached for details.* [NB: Not included in case study.]

RESULTS
No errors were found.

CONCLUSION
Invoices are correctly posted to the sales ledger.

Test 3

OBJECTIVE
To ensure that payments received from debtors are posted correctly to the sales ledger.

WORK DONE
Selected from the cash book a representative sample of 30 cheques received from debtors. Ensured that each had been
(a) posted to the correct debtor's account;
(b) matched to the invoices to which it related.
See attached for results. [NB: Not included in case study.]

RESULTS
All cheque receipts were correctly posted except:

DATE REC'D	CUSTOMER	£
15.5.X7	S. Spriggs	1,000
11.6.X7	Wareco Ltd	600

The amount from Spriggs arrived without a remittance advice so that it was not possible to establish what invoices it related to. Wareco is in financial difficulties and has agreed to pay off its balance in monthly instalments of £600. In both cases, the sales ledger clerk followed W's policy of applying unallocated amounts to the oldest balance first.

CONCLUSION
It appears that receipts are correctly posted to the sales ledger in accordance with W's policy.

Test 4

OBJECTIVE
To ensure that credit is given only to approved customers and that credit limits are not exceeded.

WORK DONE
(a) For a sample of 25 new accounts opened this year checked that 2 references had been taken up and that the credit controller had approved the level of credit given.
(b) For a sample of 25 accounts, compared credit limit with balance currently outstanding.
See attached for details. [NB: Not included in case study.]

RESULTS
(a) No references had been taken up for:
Frank Brewer Ltd. *Apparently, this customer had placed an urgent large order for shelving which would have been lost if W had insisted on references before proceeding. References were subsequently received and proved satisfactory.*
Megacorp Inc. *This US customer was recommended by a close friend of the MD.*

<u>Contadini</u>. *An Italian customer. No further explanation could be given.*

<u>Tevere</u>. *As for Contadini. Both these cos have fairly small balances.*

Otherwise, all customers selected had provided references before being given credit.

(b) On review of the sales ledger it appeared that about 40% of accounts balances exceeded the stated credit limit, so it was decided to abandon this test and discuss the situation with the credit controller. He explained that many credit limits were set years ago and have not subsequently been subjected to a formal review. W would lose customers if it held them to unrealistically low levels of credit, but he has not got the time or resources to carry out a full-scale review of old limits. He copes with this by sanctioning breaches of the limit where he is satisfied that customers are a good risk.

CONCLUSION
It appears that the company's stated policy on credit limits is not being adhered to.

Test 5

OBJECTIVE
To ensure that debtors exist and are correctly stated.

WORK DONE
Selected a sample of 25 sales ledger balances by choosing the one with the highest value for each letter of the alphabet. These represented 32% of the total sales ledger balance of £604,632 at 31 August. Wrote to the customer requesting confirmation. See attached sample letter and list of balances.

RESULTS
To be written up when replies are received.

SAMPLE DEBTORS CIRCULARIZATION LETTER

Dear Sir/Madam

According to our records, your balance with us at 31 August 19X7 was £----
due to us.

Our auditors, Thomas, Gordon & Co., wish to confirm this balance as part of their audit of our financial statements for the year ended 30 September 19X7. Would you please complete and sign the tear-off slip at the bottom of this letter and return it to our auditors in the enclosed envelope. If you disagree with the balance, please note on the slip the balance according to your records.

Thank you for your assistance.

Yours faithfully

J. BANKS
Financial accountant

I agree/disagree with the balance of £--- shown above as due from me at 31 August 19X7.

Signed ------------------
Position in company

DEBTORS CIRCULARIZED

NAME		£
1	Archer Ltd	11,234
2	Bowers Partnership	45,322
3	Chapman & Co.	1,290
4	Derek Inc.	7,864
5	Erica spa	11,543
6	Fratelli	6,543
7	Groves Ltd	3,211
8	Horrobin & Sons	9,867
9	IMD Ltd	3,345
10	Jacksonville Import Co.	5,436
11	Kleinfeld	998
12	Lovesey Ltd	4,567
13	Moroni	3,211
14	Newsome & Co.	8,760
15	O'Reilly	2,344
16	Parker Ltd	7,500
17	Quentin	1,290
18	Roberts Bros	6,155
19	Sullivan Storage	8,355
20	Tolley & Son	4,350
21	Underwood Ltd	12,346
22	Villanova	9,100
23	Walkers	6,767
24	Young Ltd	4,433
25	ZJQ Warehousing	7,651

TOTAL £193,482

7.3 Results of debtors circularization received by 1 October

(a) BALANCES AGREED

1	Archer
3	Chapman
4	Derek
6	Fratelli
7	Groves
9	IMD
11	Kleinfeld
12	Lovesey
14	Newsome
15	O'Reilly
16	Parker
17	Quentin
20	Tolley
23	Walkers

(b) DISAGREED

	£
5 Erica	
Balance per W	11,543
Cheque sent by Erica 28.8.X7	1,400
Balance per Erica	10,143
8 Horrobin	
Balance per W	9,867
Goods returned 15.8.X7 − credit requested	4,800
Balance per Horrobin	5,067
18 Roberts Bros	
Balance Per W	6,155

'This balance relates to moneys retained by us to cover any rectification work required on the warehouse installation carried out for us by W. Since the installation was completed, we have spent £7,000 on making good defects which we consider the responsibility of W. We therefore deny that £6,155 is now due to W.'

(c) NO REPLY RECEIVED

 2   Bowers*
10   Jacksonville Import Co.**
13   Moroni
19   Sullivan Storage**
21   Underwood*
22   Villanova
24   Young Ltd**
25   ZJQ Warehousing

* Both these replied that they maintain purchase ledgers in 'open item' form − i.e. they list only those invoices currently payable. They were therefore unable to state what balance was due to W at a past date.
** These are US customers.

QUESTIONS FOR DISCUSSION

1. On the basis of the results of the interim tests, what further work needs to be done in order to ensure that W's debtors are correctly stated and recoverable?
2. Comment on the basis of selection of the debtors circularization sample.
3. What further action (if any) should the auditors take in response to the results of Tests 3 and 4?

Relevant reading

Auditing Practices Committee (1989a):
   Auditing Guidelines: 2.203   Audit evidence
                     2.204   Internal controls
ICAEW Statements on Auditing and Reporting:
   5.901 Verification of debtor balances: confirmation by direct communication
Woolf (1990), pp. 122−6, 198−205, 214
Coopers & Lybrand (1985), pp. 332−47

Case 8
Britlings Brewery

BACKGROUND

Britlings Brewery (BB) is a relatively small, independent brewing company based in Sheffield, where the brewery and head office are located. Britlings owns 270 public houses in Yorkshire and Lincolnshire, all of which are run by managers. Its year-end is 31 December and its auditors are carrying out the interim audit in October 19X9 for the December 19X9 year-end.

DOCUMENTS

8.1   Summary of fixed assets at 30 September 19X9 (£000)

(i) LAND AND BUILDINGS

	Brewery and offices	Freehold and long leasehold	Short leasehold
Cost or valuation (1.1.X9)	2,000	59,000	14,000
Additions	100	11,000	300
Disposals	–	(3,000)	(1,700)
Cost or valuation (30.9.×9)	2,100	67,000	12,600
Accumulated depreciation (1.1.X9)	12	–	70
Charge for year	4	–	6
Disposals	–	–	(2)
Accumulated depreciation (30.9.X9)	16	–	74

(ii) OTHER TANGIBLE FIXED ASSETS

	Plant and equipment	Furniture & fittings	Motor vehicles
Cost at 1.1.X9	1,535	11,500	2,500
Additions	350	4,500	600
Disposals	(140)	(2,300)	(340)
Cost at 30.9.X9	1,745	13,700	2,760

Accumulated depreciation (1.1.X9)	235	825	1,500
Charge for year	85	100	520
Disposals	(25)	(50)	(290)
Accumulated depreciation (30.9.X9)	295	875	1,730

No further major additions or disposals (individually > £50,000) are scheduled to take place before the year-end.

8.2 Analysis of fixed asset movements

	£000
Additions represent:	
Brewery – enlargement of bottling area	100
Freehold and long leasehold:	
Purchase of 12 properties	7,000
Additions and refurbishments to existing properties (9 projects)	4,000
	11,000
Short leasehold – additions and refurbishments	300
Plant and equipment:	
Brewery bottling plant	190
Office computerization	70
Other items (none individually > £50,000)	90
	350
Furniture and fittings:	
Office improvements	200
Pubs – 15 major projects	3,900
Pubs – other replacements, renewals	400
	4,500
Vehicles:	
Lorries	100
Managers' cars (70 cars)	500
	600

Disposals represent:

6 freehold/long leasehold properties	3,000
8 short leaseholds	1,700
Plant and equipment:	
Old bottling plant	80
Old computer equipment	40
Sundry minor items	20
	140
Furniture and fittings − from pubs	2,300
Vehicles − 53 cars	340

8.3 Extract from Britlings Brewery's accounts for the year ended 31 December 19X8

ACCOUNTING POLICIES

Properties owned by the company are subject to valuation by chartered surveyors employed by the company. The last such valuation took place in 19X7. Other fixed assets are valued at cost.

Depreciation is provided as follows:

1. Freehold offices and industrial premises − over their estimated useful lives.
2. Freehold land − nil.
3. Freehold licensed premises − nil.
4. Leasehold land and buildings − over the terms of the leases.
5. Brewing equipment − over twenty years.
6. Other plant − over ten years.
7. Office equipment − over five years.
8. Vehicles − over five years.

It is the company's policy to maintain licensed premises in a state of repair such that the value of those properties does not diminish over time. The cost of this maintenance is charged to profits in the year in which it occurs. As a result, it is the opinion of the directors that any depreciation of licensed properties would be immaterial and accordingly no depreciation charge has been made.

8.4 Extract from permanent audit file: notes on fixed asset system

PROPERTIES

Major expenditure on properties, either the acquisition of a new pub or a large development or refurbishment project, has to be approved via a capital sanction. This is a detailed summary of the expenditure to be incurred and is prepared by the surveyor's department and approved by the board of directors. Each sanction is given a code number. See sample attached at A.

Orders for work, supplies etc. are issued by purchasing department, quoting the code number.

When individual invoices are received, they are linked with the original order and approved as follows:
Expenditure <£1,000 — surveyor
Expenditure >£1,000 — financial accountant
Expenditure >£5,000 — finance director
Expenditure >£50,000 — board of directors
and are then coded to the appropriate capital sanction. A quarterly summary is prepared by the financial accountant comparing actual with budgeted expenditure and is reviewed by the board. See B for example. All disposals of properties must be approved by the board of directors.

Each property is allotted a code number and recorded in the Estates Register, a computerized listing of properties, which records both the original purchase and the cost of additions and alterations.

All freehold property deeds and copies of lease agreements are held at head office and filed by code number. A register is kept in which details of issues and returns of deeds (e.g. to/from solicitors) are noted.

PLANT AND EQUIPMENT

This includes brewing vessels and equipment, computers and other office machinery and beer storage and dispensing equipment at pubs. A computerized fixed asset register is maintained. Every asset capitalized and not fully depreciated is included on the register, identified by a unique code number which is also recorded on the asset itself. The register also calculates depreciation.

Additions to plant and equipment must be sanctioned by the manager of the department concerned. Items costing more than £1,000 must be approved by the financial accountant and those over £5,000 by the finance director. Items over £50,000 must be sanctioned by the board of directors.

It is company policy to write off items with a value < £100 to expenses. Disposals must be sanctioned by the manager of the department concerned. Disposals of items with proceeds or net book value in excess of £5,000 must be sanctioned by the finance director.

VEHICLES

These comprise beer delivery lorries and tankers and the cars provided to pub managers and senior managers within the company. Registration documents are retained by the fleet manager, who authorizes all purchases and disposals of vehicles up to £50,000.

A: EXAMPLE OF CAPITAL SANCTION

LOCATION   King's Arms, Bruddersford

PROJECT   Extend and refurbish bars

START DATE   1 March 19X9

ESTIMATED DURATION   2 months

BUDGETED COSTS	£
Architect's fees	4,500
Building labour and materials	71,000
Plant hire	3,800
Painting and decoration	11,000
Furniture	19,000
Carpeting	4,690
Fittings	9,540
Total	123,530

B: EXAMPLE OF QUARTERLY EXPENDITURE SUMMARY

LOCATION   White Rose, Darrowby

PROJECT   Build restaurant and conservatory

START DATE   31 March 19X9

ESTIMATED DURATION   6 months

REPORT DATE   30 June 19X9

	BUDGET	ACTUAL
	£	£
Architect's fees	5,000	5,100
Building labour and materials	55,000	39,000
Plant hire	3,900	2,300
Painting and decoration	12,000	—
Furniture	20,000	—
Carpeting	7,000	—
Fittings	9,500	—
Total	112,400	46,400

QUESTIONS FOR DISCUSSION

1. Describe and evaluate the effectiveness of the company's system for controlling additions to and disposals of fixed assets.
2. Suggest tests for verifying:
   (a) that land and buildings exist and are owned by the company;
   (b) that their value is fairly stated;
   (c) that plant and equipment exists and its value is fairly stated;
   (d) that vehicles exist and are owned by the company.

Relevant reading

Auditing Practices Committee (1989a):
  Auditing Guidelines: 2.204 Internal controls
Woolf (1990), p. 92
Coopers & Lybrand (1985), pp. 247–78

Case 9
Mrs Beeton's Kitchens Limited

BACKGROUND

Mrs Beeton's Kitchens Ltd (MBK) specializes in the design and installation of fitted kitchens. Fitting consultants visit a customer's home, measure the kitchen and quote a price based on the type of units and electrical appliances selected by the customer. MBK buys in the appliances – cookers, refrigerators, dishwashers, etc. – from the manufacturers, and also buys fittings such as sinks and taps. It makes the kitchen units, counters and shelves in its own workshop. A kitchen can cost from £3,000 to £10,000, depending on the type and number of units and appliances installed. Customers are required to pay a 20 per cent deposit when they place their order, and the balance is payable when the work is completed. It is July 19X9 and MBK's auditors are currently carrying out the audit for the year ending 30 June 19X9.

DOCUMENTS

9.1 Draft summary of creditors and accruals for the year ended 30 June 19X9

	19X9 £	19X8 £
Purchase ledger balance	359,087	238,566
Bank overdraft	100,235	76,897
Bank loan	25,000	–
Accruals:		
Goods received not invoiced*	84,950	100,500
PAYE and NI	37,000	29,000
VAT	55,000	39,000
Light and heat	30,000	37,000
Telephone	3,000	2,300
Sundry	11,000	21,000
Customer deposits received	16,500	12,500
	721,772	556,763

* Stores dept makes a list of items received in the last week of the financial year for which invoices are unlikely to be received until after the balance sheet date. The estimated value of those items is used as a basis for the 'goods received not invoiced' figure.

9.2 Draft profit and loss account for the year ended 30 June 19X9

	19X9	19X8
	£000	£000
Turnover	10,400	7,300
Wages	3,200	2,900
Materials	1,230	1,000
Appliances	3,000	2,000
Fittings	420	220
Gross profit	2,550	1,180
Salaries	600	450
Light and heat	230	180
Depreciation	220	190
Telephone and stationery	100	70
Motor expenses	110	80
Interest and bank charges	70	45
	1,220	165

9.3 Purchase ledger systems notes

1.   An order is raised by the Buying Department, based on a requisition from the department requiring the item. The order is sequentially numbered and produced in a carbon set with 4 copies:
— top copy to supplier
— copy retained by Buying Dept
— copy to department making the requisition
— copy to goods receiving department
Managers are subject to authority limits in signing order requisitions. Individual limits are:
— departmental manager: £5,000
— financial director: £20,000
— managing director: £50,000
— main board: all amounts over £50,000

2.   When the goods are received, the accompanying delivery note is compared with the order to ensure the goods are correct and is marked with the order number. The order is then stamped 'GOODS RECEIVED' and sent to the purchase ledger department and filed there in number order. The delivery note is sent to the Buying Department and filed there in alphabetical order of supplier name.

3.   The supplier's invoice is sent to the purchase ledger department where it is matched with the stamped order. (Suppliers are requested to quote MBK's order number on their invoices.) A purchase ledger clerk reviews the invoice to check that:

− price, type and quantity of goods invoiced agree with order;
− supplier is one of the company's authorized suppliers;
− the invoice is arithmetically correct.

The clerk then initials the invoice to indicate approval and enters on it the relevant purchase ledger and nominal ledger codes to which it is to be posted. If an invoice is denominated in a foreign currency, she translates it into £ sterling at the prevailing exchange rate for the day on which she processes it.

Where no purchase order exists, e.g. for utilities or professional services, the invoice is passed to the departmental manager concerned, who signs it to indicate authorization (subject to the limits noted in 1 above) and returns it.

4. The invoice is then passed to the data input clerk, who enters it into the computer in accordance with the codes indicated and returns it to purchase ledger department for filing in alphabetical order of supplier.

5. When the invoice is input, it simultaneously updates:
− the purchase ledger
− the nominal ledger
− the purchase invoice listing.

6. Once a month, the computer produces a listing of purchase ledger balances, showing the amount payable to each supplier and the invoices making it up. The financial accountant reviews the listing and marks on it the amounts to be paid to each supplier, e.g. the whole amount, all invoices more than 2 months old, etc. This is done in order to optimize the company's cash position by paying creditors only when it is desirable or essential, e.g. in order to obtain discounts or to ensure further orders are accepted.

7. The marked listing is then passed to the cashier, who inputs the information to the computer. The computer run:
− prints cheques to the suppliers concerned;
− prints a remittance advice, to be sent out with the cheque, stating which invoices it is paying;
− updates the cash book;
− updates the purchase ledger;
− updates the cash account in the nominal ledger.

The cheques are signed by the financial director and sent out with remittance advices.

8. Until November 19X8, a purchase ledger clerk compared purchase ledger balances with the monthly statements sent out by suppliers and followed up any discrepancies. When the clerk left, she was not replaced, and there is currently no review of suppliers' statements.

9. If goods are returned to a supplier because they are defective, they are accompanied by a goods return note. This is sequentially numbered and recorded in a goods return book which shows the goods involved, their order number and the supplier to whom they were returned. The stamped order copy is attached to the carbon of the goods return note and both are retained

in the stores until a replacement for the goods is received, when the order is processed as described in 2 above.

9.4 Summary of purchase ledger balances at 30 June 19X9

BALANCES INDIVIDUALLY >£10,000:

	Notes	£
Ruritanian Electrical	*1*	*100,090*
Breckland Timber		*45,800*
Perrys Plumbing Supplies		*12,346*
Plastitops Ltd		*15,500*
Ace Carpentry Supplies		*16,754*
Lave-Vaisselle	*2*	*68,765*
Freezomat Refrigerators		*28,760*
		288,015
75 other balances		*71,072*
(largest £9,000, smallest £3)		
		359,087

NOTES
1. *MBK imports all the cookers it sells from Ruritania. Ruritanian Electrical invoices it in the local currency, the rudolf. MBK cannot buy rudolfs forward, as a result of exchange restrictions. During the year, the value of the rudolf has increased from £1 = 50R to £1 = 40R.*
2. *Lave-Vaisselle is a French company which supplies MBK with dishwashers. It invoices MBK in £ sterling.*

9.5 Extract from systems audit working papers for the year ended 30 June 19X9

Purchases Test 1

Objective: *To ensure that recorded liabilities represent goods or services which have been received by the company.*

Work done: *Selected a representative sample of 30 purchase invoices posted to the purchase ledger between July 19X8 and June 19X9. For each invoice, ensured that:*
— *the invoice had been initialled by the purchase ledger clerk*
— *the invoice details were in agreement with the copy order*
— *the copy order had been stamped 'GOODS RECEIVED'*
or, where the invoice was for services, ensured that it had been approved by an authorized person.

Results: *See attached for details.* [NB: Not included in case study.] *No errors were found.*

Conclusion: *Recorded liabilities represent goods or services which have been received by the company.*

Test 2

Objective: *To ensure that goods or services cannot be received without a liability being recorded.*

Work done: *Selected a representative sample of 30 delivery notes from those filed in the Buying Dept and ensured that the liability to which they related had been posted to the purchase ledger. This was done by tracing details from delivery notes held in Buying Dept to orders, thence to stamped orders and invoices and tracing the invoices to the purchase ledger, ensuring that the correct amount had been posted to the correct supplier and in the correct period.*

Results:

	SUPPLIER	DELIVERY DATE	INVOICE SEEN	POSTED TO P.L.
1	Perrys	1 July	Y	Y
2	Abco	16 July	Y	Y
3	Ace	29 July	Y	Y
4	Walker	5 Aug	Y	Y
5	Freezo	13 Aug	Y	Y
6	Martin	28 Aug	Y	Y
7	Premier	3 Sept	Y	Y
8	Bird Ltd	11 Sept	Y	Y
9	McBride	19 Sept	Y	Y
10	Hayes Ltd	1 Oct	Y	Y
11	Perks & Co	20 Oct	Y	Y
12	Tompkins	29 Oct	Y	Y
13	James Ltd	3 Nov	Y	Y
14	Porter	17 Nov	Y	Y
15	Jessop plc	2 Dec	Y	Y
16	SJ Industries	22 Dec	Y	Y
17	Ruritanian	7 Jan	Y	Y
18	Mead	30 Jan	Y	Y
19	Shearer Ltd	8 Feb	Y	Y
20	O'Ryan	16 Feb	Y	Y

21	Khan Ltd	14 Mar	Y	Y
22	Campbell	29 Mar	Y	Y
23	Franklin & Co.	4 Apr	Y	Y
24	Henry	13 Apr	N	N
25	XL Products	6 May	Y	Y
26	Breckland	17 May	Y	Y
27	Plastitops	31 May	Y	N
28	Miller Bros	11 Jun	Y	Y
29	PK Plumbing	14 Jun	Y	N
30	Lave-Vaisselle	26 Jun	N	N

(Y = yes, N = no)

'No' answers can be explained as follows:

Henry — *purchase ledger dept have investigated this and have come to the conclusion that the invoice must have been mislaid. They will write to the supplier and request a duplicate.*

Plastitops — *this invoice has not been posted to the purchase ledger because of a query by MBK about the price charged. It will be posted when the price has been agreed with the supplier.*

PK Plumbing — *the invoice is still (20 July) with the Contracts Manager for approval.*

Lave-Vaisselle — *invoice not yet received. Apparently there is normally a delay of 4 weeks between Lave-Vaisselle's delivery of goods and sending an invoice.*

[...]

QUESTIONS FOR DISCUSSION

1. Test 2 above is incomplete. Suggest what conclusions the auditor might have drawn from it.
2. What final audit tests might be performed to test whether the following are completely and correctly stated:
   (a) purchase ledger balance;
   (b) bank overdraft;
   (c) bank loan;
   (d) goods received not invoiced?

Relevant reading

Auditing Practices Committee (1989a):
   Auditing Guidelines: 4.401   Bank reports for audit purposes
Coopers & Lybrand (1985), pp. 364—87
Woolf (1990), pp. 213—14

Case 10
Golden Foods Limited

BACKGROUND

Golden Foods (GF) Ltd makes pies, pastries and pizzas, which it sells to retailers under its own brand-name and also supplies to a major supermarket chain. It has two sites: the bakery and its head office at Darlington, and a distribution depot in Wolverhampton.

GF's year-end is 31 March 19X9 and its accounts are required to be ready for publication by 30 May. It is now 19 May and the final audit work is due to be completed by 20 May. The manager in charge of the audit is reviewing the audit file with a view to identifying any unresolved problems.

(You may assume that an interim audit has been performed, and that its results were satisfactory except for any deficiencies specifically mentioned in the case study.)

DOCUMENTS

10.1 Summary of results

	19X9	19X8
	£000	£000
Turnover	3,768	3,477
Gross profit	1,240	1,199
Gross profit %	32.9	34.5
Net profit	208	189
Fixed assets	1,100	1,005
Stock	140	195
Debtors	712	597
Bank balances	43	51
Current liabilities	(433)	(494)
Net assets	1,562	1,354
Share capital	1,100	1,100
Reserves	462	254
Shareholders' funds	1,562	1,354

73

10.2 Stock summary

	19X9 £000	19X8 £000
At Darlington:		
Finished products	43	61
Raw materials	41	48
Packing materials	38	47
At Wolverhampton:		
Finished products	18	39
Total	140	195

NOTES:
The following audit work has been carried out on the stock at Darlington:
— *attended physical stocktake held on 31 March and performed test counts;*
— *ensured that material items of stock had been valued at the lower of cost and net realizable value;*
— *ensured that none of the stock on hand at 31 March was damaged or out of condition.*
The results of all tests were satisfactory.

Because of staff shortages, a physical count was not performed at Wolverhampton. The stock figure was extracted from the stock records maintained at the depot. The audit team paid a one-day visit to the Wolverhampton depot, in the course of which it performed the following audit work:
— *agreed the stock balance in the accounts to the stock records;*
— *discussed the year-end stock figure with the depot manager and ascertained that he considered the figure to be reasonable and that in his opinion year-end stock did not require any provision for obsolete/damaged items.*

10.3 Summary of debtors

	19X9 £000	19X8 £000
Trade debtors	535	498
Loan to related company	120	20
Prepayments	57	79
Total	712	597

10.4   Summary of results of debtors circularization

WORK DONE

A sample of 48 debtors was circularized. This represented all balances
>£10,000 at 31 March and a representative sample of 25 others. A
reminder letter was sent to all who had not replied by 1 May.

RESULTS

Results were as follows, on the basis of replies received up to 18
May.

	Notes	£000	No.	% of value
Agreed		109	18	30
Reconciled	1	140	14	37
Disagreed	2	31	1	8
No reply		95	15	25
Total		375	48	100

NOTES:

1.   Reconciling items were due to differences between the dates at
which invoices and payments were entered in customers' and in GF's
records.

2.   The disagreement relates to an invoice for £3,000 sent to this
customer in December 19X8. The customer is refusing to pay, on the
grounds that the goods were damaged in transit.

CONCLUSION

As only £109K of debtor balances out of a total of £535K have been
confirmed, it is not possible to conclude whether or not debtors are
correctly stated.

10.5   Loan to associated company

This is an unsecured loan made to Bartleby Ltd, a company in which
GF owns 10% of the share capital. GF loaned Bartleby £20K in 19X8 to
provide working capital, and this amount has now been increased to
£120K. No repayments have been received. The finance director of GF
was unwilling for us to include this balance in our circulation of
debtors. Accordingly, audit work has been confined to the following:

— agreed balance outstanding to the nominal ledger;
— traced payment to cash book, bank statement and returned cheque
 and ensured the cheque payee is Bartleby;
— discussed the balance with Mrs Bateman, the finance director, who
 stated that in her opinion it is fully recoverable.

10.6   Fixed assets

All figures £000

COST	1.4.X8	Addns	Disposals	31.3.X9
Freehold land & buildings	600	200	–	800
Plant	2,000	1,000	700	2,300
Motor vehicles	300	700	200	800
Fixtures & fittings	105	200	5	300
Total	3,005	2,100	905	4,200

DEPRECIATION	1.4.X8	For year	Disposals	31.3.X9
Freehold buildings	125	20	–	145
Plant	1,575	850	60	2,365
Motor vehicles	250	250	35	465
Fixtures & fittings	50	80	5	125
Total	2,000	1,200	100	3,100

NET BOOK VALUE	1,005			1,100

Notes
(1) The addition to land and buildings is in fact the surplus arising on revaluation. This revaluation was carried out by one of the directors of GF, who is a chartered surveyor.
(2) The figure for additions to plant has been overstated. A number of orders for items of plant not received at the year-end have been accrued instead of being treated as capital commitments. As a result, fixed assets and current liabilities have both been overstated by £75K.

QUESTIONS FOR DISCUSSION

Assuming that the results of the audit were satisfactory in all other areas:

1. Identify the unresolved problems which the audit manager has to clear. What is the potential impact of each on the financial statements?
2. Suggest how each of the problems might be resolved by the audit team and/or GF's management in the time available. The alternatives might include:
   (a) altering the accounts;

(b) qualifying the audit report;
(c) obtaining management assurances in the letter of representation performing additional audit work.

In each case you should be specific about the steps to be taken (e.g. what tests are to be performed, what audit qualification is needed, etc.).

Relevant reading

Auditing Practices Committee (1989a):
    Auditing Guidelines: 4.404   Representations by management
                   4.413   Reliance on other specialists
Auditing Practices Committee (1989b)
Woolf (1990), pp. 218–23
Coopers & Lybrand (1985), pp. 259–61, 302–10, 385–6

Case 11
Massive Motors Limited

BACKGROUND

Massive Motors Ltd (MM) is part of the Massive Group plc, which has a consolidated turnover of £200 million. MM operates a chain of garages throughout the UK which sell petrol and carry out repairs and services. Three of the garages also deal in new and second-hand cars. MM is a UK dealer for Eagle cars, which are imported from Ruthenia. Its year-end is 31 March.

Jill White is the audit partner in charge of the MM audit. The 19X8 audit fieldwork has just been completed, and Jill is reviewing the file in order to establish whether any additional work needs to be done and to identify matters for discussion with MM's financial director at their closing audit meeting, which is due to be held tomorrow.

DOCUMENTS

11.1   Draft summarized accounts for MM for the year ended 31 March 19X8

	£000
TURNOVER:	
Petrol	6,140
Repairs and services	1,500
Car sales	4,350
TOTAL	11,990
COST OF SALES	7,300
GROSS MARGIN	4,690
EXPENSES	2,150
NET PROFIT BEFORE TAX	2,540
FIXED ASSETS	
Land & buildings	4,500
Plant	1,200
Fixtures & fittings	500
Vehicles	600
	6,800

CURRENT ASSETS
Stock	4,075
Debtors & prepayments	1,640
Bank & cash	125
	5,840

CURRENT LIABILITIES
Creditors & accruals	1,100
Bank loan	3,000
	4,100

NET CURRENT ASSETS	1,740
NET ASSETS	8,540

REPRESENTED BY:
Share capital	5,000
Profit & loss account	2,540
Revaluation reserve	1,000
	8,540

11.2 Extract from 19X8 audit file

LAND AND BUILDINGS

MM owns 5 freehold garages and its head office building in Barchester; it does not own any leaseholds. Land and buildings are valued in the balance sheet on the basis of an independent valuation carried out by a firm of surveyors in 19X7. Values of individual sites are as follows:

	£000
Barchester	875
Stoke	1,050
Cardiff	760
Dundee	635
Bristol	580
Leeds	600
Total	4,500

Recently (June 19X8), MM's management has commissioned another independent valuation. They do not intend to incorporate the results in the 19X8 financial statements as they were notified after the year-end. The revaluation is summarized below.

	£000
Barchester	*975*
Stoke	*850*
Cardiff	*1,060*
Dundee	*785*
Bristol	*980*
Leeds	*650*
Total	*5,300*

At 31 March, MM had contracted with Newtown Properties plc to purchase a site in Newtown and with the Betta Building Co. Ltd for the construction of a garage and car showroom there. The site is expected to cost £500K and the building work c. £275K.

11.3 Extracts from minutes of the meeting of the board of directors of MM Ltd, held on 31 March 19X8 at MM House, Barchester

Agenda Item 6: Capital investments

On receiving a report from the Capital Investment Subcommittee, the board authorized the purchase of the following:

	Authorized price £
1 breakdown recovery lorry	10,000
3 Ford Sierra cars for sales managers	30,000
Equipment for installation at Cardiff, as specified on attached schedule	18,000

Agenda Item 7: Legal claim by Identical Copiers Ltd

The company secretary reported that he had contacted the company's solicitors on 24 March, and they had confirmed that Identical Copiers were proceeding with their claim for damages against MM. The solicitors recommended that MM should proceed to give them instructions so that they could proceed as soon as possible with their related case against Flitwick Motor Spares Ltd. After some discussion, it was agreed that the company secretary, together with Mr Goodwood, the Operations Director, should prepare a detailed report for discussion at the next board meeting.

Agenda Item 10: Guarantee to Caledonian Bank Ltd

The seal of the company was affixed to a guarantee given to the Caledonian Bank Ltd by the company in respect of the £1.5M loan made by the Bank to Massive Manufacturing Ltd.

11.4 Extract from 19X8 audit file: note of a meeting with Mr Alan Chivers, Company Secretary of MM Ltd, on 15 March 19X8

PRESENT: A. Chivers — Company Secretary
            B. Bryant — Audit Senior

I explained that I had asked to see Mr Chivers in order to discuss the possible existence of any outstanding legal matters which needed to be reflected in MM's accounts. Mr Chivers stated that as company secretary he was responsible for all the company's legal affairs. The only matter currently outstanding was the suit for damages being brought against the company by Identical Copiers (IC) of Bristol.

IC was a small company which provided a copier repair service and guaranteed that all customers within 25 miles of Bristol city centre would receive a visit from an IC repairman within 2 hours of calling the company. IC used a fleet of 5 vans to call on customers.

In the first week of October 19X7, the MM garage in Bristol carried out a service and overhaul of all IC's vans. In the fortnight that followed, all the vans successively broke down. They proved to need major engine repairs, which meant that IC was without any vans for 2 working days and operating with a skeleton fleet for a further 5 days. During this time, IC was unable to honour its guarantee of service within 2 hours. As a result, it lost several customers, including a major customer to whom it had made 30% of its sales in its first year of trading. IC went into liquidation in January 19X8 as a result of the losses it had sustained.

Mr Frank Thorn, the managing director of IC and its major shareholder, is suing MM for damages of £250K. He claims that the company's liquidation was caused by the loss of its fleet of vans and that the vans had been damaged by MM's installation of defective parts when they carried out the service in October 19X7. MM's costs are estimated at £30K.

MM does not dispute the facts of the case. It considers, however, that the ultimate liability for the damage suffered by IC lies with Flitwick Motor Spares Ltd, from whom it purchased the parts used on the IC vehicles. MM intends to bring a claim for damages against Flitwick for their negligence in supplying defective parts, and this claim will be for the amount of damages claimed by IC together with MM's own legal costs.

Mr Chivers considers that there is no need for MM to disclose IC's claim in the 19X8 accounts, as the likely outcome of the cases will have a net effect of nil on MM's results — the damages paid to IC will be balanced out by those recovered from Flitwick. He also considers that disclosure would be damaging to MM, both by prejudging the outcome of the IC case, which could conceivably go in MM's favour, and by giving Flitwick advance warning that MM intends to bring an action against them.

11.5 Reply to bank confirmation request sent by auditors

30 April 19X8

Dear Sirs

MASSIVE MOTORS LTD

In response to your letter dated 2 April 19X8, we wish to report the following in respect of our above customer:

BANK ACCOUNTS IN CUSTOMER'S NAME:
A/C No. 10009876: Balance at 31 March 19X8 100,000 Ruthenian dinars

No other accounts in this name existed during the year.

CUSTOMER'S ASSETS HELD AS SECURITY:
None

CUSTOMER'S OTHER ASSETS HELD:
None

CONTINGENT LIABILITIES:
Outstanding forward foreign exchange contracts:
£100,000 for delivery of 50,000 Ruthenian dinars on 1 July 19X8
£100,000 for delivery of 55,000 Ruthenian dinars on 1 September 19X8

This reply is given solely for the purpose of your audit without any responsibility to you on the part of the bank, its employees or agents, but it is not to relieve you from any other inquiry or from the performance of any other duty.

Yours faithfully

R. Singh
Manager, Cheapside Branch

Audit note: at 31 March 19X8, £1 = 0.5 Ruthenian dinar

11.6 Extract from 19X8 audit file: contingent liabilities

As a promotional exercise, MM gave a 12-month warranty on all second-hand cars it sold during the year ending 31 March 19X8. Under the warranty, it will provide free repairs on all cars it supplied (with the exclusion of repairs to windscreens and tyres) in respect of any defect arising within 12 months of the date of sale.

During 19X7/8 MM sold 1,500 used cars, representing a turnover of £4.5M. According to its costing records, which we have reviewed, the average cost of a repair job (comprising labour, parts and allocation of overhead but excluding any mark-up) was £125.

MM proposes to disclose this as a contingent liability in the notes to the accounts.

QUESTIONS FOR DISCUSSION

1. Identify the issues in these working papers which might be described as:
   (a) post-balance sheet events;
   (b) commitments;
   (c) contingencies.
2. For each issue, comment on:
   (a) the accounting treatment/disclosure proposed by MM. Do you consider it to be correct? If not, what treatment/disclosure would you suggest?
   (b) the audit work done. Is it adequate? If not, what additional work do you consider necessary?

Relevant reading

Auditing Practices Committee (1989a):
    Auditing Guidelines: 4.401 Bank reports for audit purposes
                      4.402 Events after the balance sheet date
ICAEW Statements on Auditing and Reporting:
    5.906 The ascertainment and confirmation of contingent liabilities arising from pending legal matters
Auditing Standards Committee (1989):
    SSAP 17 Accounting for post balance sheet events
    SSAP 18 Accounting for contingencies
Coopers & Lybrand (1985), pp. 374–5, 831–5, 407–10
Woolf (1990), pp. 249–71

Case 12
Holiday Holdings Limited

BACKGROUND

Holiday Holdings Ltd (HH) is a group of companies in the leisure industry. Its subsidiaries include Lyndon Hotel Ltd and the Park Leisure Complex Ltd.

Because of pressure on audit fees, the auditors of HH are anxious to reduce the time taken to carry out their substantive audit testing during the 19X9 audit. One means of doing this which they wish to use is that of analytical review. The audit senior, Susan Grey, has collected data on two areas which she considers suitable for analytical review: turnover for room lettings at the hotel, and wages and salaries at the leisure complex.

DOCUMENTS

12.1 Lyndon Hotel: Extract from permanent audit file

The hotel has 3 main sources of income: the bar, the restaurant and room lettings. It maintains separate cash and nominal accounts for all these activities. Where a guest's bill includes charges for two different categories, e.g. room and bar, the sales are subsequently re-analysed by the hotel's accountant to post the appropriate amounts to the correct accounts.

The hotel has 100 bedrooms, all of which are double rooms, but which are also let for single occupancy. The room rate for 19X9 is £25 if the room is let to one person and £30 if it is let to two people. The fact that the room rate is higher for double than for single occupancy makes it important that guests are correctly invoiced, i.e. that a room occupied by two people is charged at the double rate. The receptionist who prepares the invoice for a guest on departure is required to check the rate charged against the booking confirmation, to ensure that the correct rate has been used.

In addition to a monthly profit and loss account, the hotel accountant produces statistics for management information which show room occupancy, i.e. the % of rooms used, and bed occupancy, i.e. the average use of beds during the month. For instance:

Available bed nights in May = 31 days × 200 beds = 6,200

If 2,540 bed nights were sold, May occupancy = 41%

If all rooms are let for single occupancy, the maximum bed occupancy is 50%.

These statistics are based on the data taken at the time of booking, not on the invoiced amounts.

12.2 Summary of occupancy statistics for year ending 30 April 19X9

	Room occupancy %	Bed occupancy %
May	65	41
June	67	48
July	71	56
August	70	51
September	65	52
October	63	47
November	60	44
December	57	45
January	57	46
February	61	52
March	58	43
April	63	47
Annual average	63	47.67

12.3 Extract from profit and loss account for the year ended 30 April 19X9

	19X9 £	19X8 £
TURNOVER		
Bar	435,000	400,987
Restaurant	367,589	349,876
Room letting	622,710	600,321
Total	1,425,299	1,351,184

12.4 Park Leisure Complex Ltd: Extract from 19X9 audit file

Park employs 50 weekly-paid and 10 monthly-paid (salaried) staff. Park has a pension scheme for its salaried employees, for whom it pays contributions calculated as 5% of their gross salary. There is no pension scheme for weekly-paid employees.

Weekly-paid employees are paid in cash. The payroll supervisor cashes the payroll cheque on Thursday of each week and pay packets are made up by her assistant to be distributed on Friday. Salaried employees are paid by bank transfer.

Both weekly- and monthly-paid employees received a 5% pay increase with immediate effect from 1 August 19X8.

The employer's national insurance contribution was 10.5% of earnings (excluding pension contributions) throughout the year.

Gross pay for a sample pay period was as follows:

Weekly-paid: week ending 7 May 19X8 £3,000 (including overtime).

Salaried: month ending 31 May 19X8 £4,580 (no overtime is payable to salaried staff).

The total cost of wages and salaries, including pension contributions and employer's NI, was £256,000 for the year ending 30 April 19X9.

QUESTIONS FOR DISCUSSION

1. Using the information given in the documents above:
   (a) Estimate the expected level of
      (i) income from room lettings;
      (ii) wages and salaries,
      for Lyndon and Park for the year ended 30 April 19X9.
   (b) Compare your results with the actual reported figures and suggest reasons for the difference.
   (c) What are the advantages and drawbacks of an analytical review approach to substantive testing?

Relevant reading

Auditing Practices Committee (1989a):
   Auditing Guidelines: 4.417   Analytical review
Coopers & Lybrand (1985), pp. 210–13
Woolf (1990), pp. 240–9

Case 13
Fantasy Fashions Limited

PEOPLE INVOLVED

Pinkerton & Co.
Arun Desai: Audit Partner
Jane Banks: Audit Manager
Sue Lloyd: Trainee

Fantasy Fashions Ltd
Jim Green: Managing Director
Paul Stevens: Accountant

BACKGROUND

Fantasy is a small company manufacturing clothes which it sells wholesale. It has few accounting systems, so the audit tends to be largely substantive. Sue Lloyd has completed her work on the accounts prepared by Paul Stevens. Paul is accurate and conscientious, but tends to leave any accounting policy decisions to Jim Green, who is a much more forceful character.

DOCUMENTS

13.1 Pinkerton & Co. − Internal memo

From   Jane Banks   *8 February 1988*
To   Sue Lloyd

FANTASY FASHIONS LTD
I looked at the files over the weekend. It all seems OK to me, apart from stock. Can you write me a short note about those T-shirts?

Thanks
Jane

13.2 Pinkerton & Co. − Internal memo

To   Jane
From   Sue

Here's a few notes on stock. Hope they're what you wanted.
*   Sue*

FANTASY FASHIONS LTD
Year ended 31.12.87

STOCK SUMMARY

	1987 £	1986 £
Raw materials:		
cotton	3,060	2,179
jersey	1,075	1,535
thread, zips, etc.	1,013	1,853
Finished goods:		
jeans	–	3,599
overalls	–	6,900
T-shirts*	39,000	–
	44,148	16,066

* These are 19,500 T-shirts which have been in stock since April 1987, when they were made for Giant Stores. I have inspected them during the stocktake, and they appear to be well made and in good condition. According to Mr Stevens, the accountant, they were rejected by Giant because the dye did not match other items in Giant's 1987 summer range. After an exchange of letters and visits lasting until September, Fantasy gave up the attempt to persuade Giant to pay for the T-shirts and accepted that they were not up to the standard specified in the original agreement because of the dye fault.

Fantasy did not try to find an alternative buyer during the summer, in the hope that Giant would relent. Mr Stevens tells me that a number of customers have expressed an interest in the garments this year, but he admits that no firm orders have yet been placed.

The T-shirts cost about 90p each to make, according to Mr Stevens. They are valued in the balance sheet at £2 each, which was the agreed selling price to Giant.

13.3 Fantasy Fashions Ltd: Profit and loss account for the year ended 31 December 1987

	1987 £	1986 £
Turnover	181,640	176,132
Operating costs	161,213	149,137

Operating profit	20,427	26,995
Interest payable	300	–
Profit before tax	20,127	26,995
Taxation	8,000	9,500
RETAINED PROFIT	12,127	17,495

RETAINED RESERVES

At 1 January 1987	40,116	22,621
Profit for 1987	12,127	17,495
At 31 December	52,243	40,116

13.4 Fantasy Fashions Ltd: Balance sheet at 31 December 1987

	1987	1986
	£	£
FIXED ASSETS	33,500	25,000
CURRENT ASSETS		
Stock	44,148	16,066
Debtors	6,520	16,300
Bank and cash	750	13,000
	51,418	45,366
CURRENT LIABILITIES		
Bank overdraft	5,000	–
Trade creditors	9,675	10,750
Taxation	8,000	9,500
	22,675	20,250
Net current assets	28,743	25,116
Net assets	62,243	50,116
REPRESENTED BY		
Share capital	10,000	10,000
Reserves	52,243	40,116
	62,243	50,116

13.5   Pinkerton & Co. – Internal memo

From   *Jane Banks*
To   *Arun Desai*   *10 February 1988*

FANTASY FASHIONS LTD
As you suggested, I went to see Jim Green, the managing director of
Fantasy, yesterday to discuss stock valuation. Unfortunately, he went
up the wall as soon as I mentioned it. When he had calmed down a bit,
he made the following points:

1.   Giant has abused its dominant position by refusing to take up the
T-shirts. If Fantasy had the resources, it would sue Giant and compel it
to honour the contract. The difference between the dye quality specified
and the actual colour of the T-shirts is tiny.

2.   If Fantasy had not wasted last summer negotiating with Giant, it
would have been able to find another buyer for the T-shirts and this
problem of year-end valuation would not have arisen.

3.   As director of Fantasy, he is in any case better placed than the
auditors to determine the value of his stock. He regards any questioning
of his valuation as a sign that we do not trust him. He strongly hinted
that he would consider a change of auditor if we could not 'reach an
acceptable solution' – which I take to mean agreement to use his
valuation.

Anyway, I am leaving you the files, and will be grateful for your
comments.

Jane

13.6   Pinkerton & Co. – Internal memo

FROM   *Arun Desai*
TO   *Jane Banks*   *15 February 1988*

FANTASY FASHIONS
Thank you for letting me see the files. Can you and Sue come to my
office at 9.15 tomorrow? We need to discuss our next step.

A.D.

QUESTIONS FOR DISCUSSION

1. What further audit work, if any, should Pinkerton & Co. carry out before drafting their audit report?
2. What should the wording of the audit report be and why?

Relevant reading

Auditing Practices Committee (1989b)
Auditing Standards Committee (1989):
  SSAP 9   Stocks and long-term contracts
Woolf (1990), pp. 272−331

Case 14
Brighter Alloys Limited

BACKGROUND

Brighter Alloys Ltd (BA), a company based in the city of Bruddersford, deals in alloys used in the steel industry. It was founded in 1969 by Jack Brightman. In 1979 he and his family sold their shares in the company to Dickens Steel plc, and BA is now a wholly owned subsidiary of Dickens. Parker & Co. act as auditors of all the twelve companies in the Dickens Group, whose year-end is 31 December. From 1969 until 1987 Slott & Co., a small firm, were auditors of BA; the change of auditor was the decision of the finance director of Dickens.

DOCUMENTS

14.1 Summary accounts of Brighter Alloys 1986−1988

PROFIT AND LOSS ACCOUNT

£000	1986	1987	1988 (draft)
Turnover	2,150	2,325	2,200
Cost of sales	1,550	1,675	2,300
Gross margin	600	650	(100)
Admin expenses	100	108	120
Distribution expenses	147	160	170
Net profit/(loss)	353	382	(390)
Taxation	127	140	−
Profit/(loss) after tax	226	242	(390)
Dividend	175	200	−
Retained profit/(loss)	51	42	(390)

BALANCE SHEET

	1986	1987	1988
TANGIBLE FIXED ASSETS	700	720	740

CURRENT ASSETS

Stocks	675	712	120
Debtors	300	350	365
Bank and cash	50	50	15
	1,025	1,112	500

CURRENT LIABILITIES

Trade creditors	480	508	528
Overdraft	30	60	70
Taxation	150	132	–
Dividend	75	100	–
	735	800	598

Net current assets	290	312	(98)
Net assets	990	1,032	642

REPRESENTED BY

Share capital	500	500	500
Profit & loss account	490	532	142
	990	1,032	642

14.2 Note on attendance at the stocktake of Brighter Alloys Ltd, 31 December 1988

I attended the stocktake of Brighter Alloys (BA), which took place on 31 December 1988, beginning at 9.00 a.m. BA's stock is kept at two locations. Scrap is kept in the yard outside BA's offices in Dundee Street. Alloy stores are held in a warehouse in Aberdeen Street, about half a mile from the offices. I arrived at Dundee Street at 8.30 a.m., and met Mrs Glenda White, the financial accountant of Dickens. She told me that she was attending the stocktake in the place of Jim Lodge, the managing director of BA, who was unwell. He had telephoned her the previous evening to say that he would not be present.

The stocktake was carried out by professional stocktakers from Sharp & Co.; Mr Lodge had offered BA staff to perform the work, but his offer had been rejected by Peter Hart, the new financial director of Dickens, who had requested the stocktake. Mr Hart felt that BA staff had insufficient stocktaking experience. Two teams of stocktakers were in action, one at each site where stock was held. Mrs White and I went to Aberdeen Street to observe the alloy stores count, which was expected to represent most of the stock value.

Alloy stores were held in drums, each containing half a tonne. The stocktakers at Aberdeen Street had selected a random sample of drums to be moved to one end of the yard so that their lids could be cut off and the contents inspected. When we arrived, the stocktaker immediately informed us that the first drum opened, which was labelled Monel 400, had proved to contain scrap and swarf with a thin top layer of Monel. The warehouse employee present could not offer any explanation for this. Two other drums opened also proved to be full of swarf.

The stocktakers had been provided with copies of BA's most recent stock figures as a basis for conducting the count. One of them commented that there appeared to be far fewer drums on site than the stock listing would suggest, and asked Mrs White if there had been substantial sales during late December which had not yet been entered in the stock records. She said that December sales had, in fact, been extremely poor, and that she could think of no reason for the apparent stock shortage. At this point, Mrs White telephoned Mr Hart and informed him of the problems that had been encountered. She suggested that the stocktakers be instructed to open and sample all sealed drums, and that all movements in and out of the warehouse be suspended until this had been done. He agreed with this approach and work proceeded accordingly. I remained on site for the rest of the day to observe the work being carried out. Because of the need to carry out analysis of samples, the stocktakers were unable to report a stock value until a week after the initial count.

The results of the stocktakers' work as notified to Dickens on 9 January can be summarized as follows:

	£000
Value of stock per latest stock listing	695
Value of stock as counted on 31 December	120
Shortfall	575
Reasons for shortfall:	
Stock on list not found at stocktake	330
Drums found to be wholly/partly filled with swarf and scrap	120
Stock found to be of lower specification than stated in stock records*	125
	575

* This was found during the sampling process. Details are given in full on the stocktaker's report, but the main differences were as follows:

Stainless 18−8 (£1,250/tonne) instead of stainless 316 (£2,000/tonne) Monel 400 (£7,500/tonne) instead of Monel K-500 (£9,000/tonne).

14.3   Extract from *Bruddersford Daily Record*, 15 September 1989

I STOLE HALF A MILLION, ADMITS EX-STEEL BOSS LODGE

Jim Lodge, ex-managing director of Bruddersford steel firm Brighter Alloys, today pleaded guilty to defrauding his employers, Dickens Steel, of sums totalling more than half a million over the five years he had worked for them.

Lodge admitted to a series of frauds against Dickens which began shortly after his appointment to their subsidiary, Brighter Alloys. Lodge was responsible for keeping the company's books and used his position of trust to carry out a variety of frauds that benefited him, his friends and family. Local dealers Victory Metal Co., whose director Martin Thorn has already been sentenced for his part in the fraud, supplied Lodge with invoices for short or non-existent deliveries. Lodge authorized the invoices and passed them to Dickens for payment. Later, he and Thorn split Dickens's payments between them.

As Lodge found that this went unnoticed, he began to submit fake invoices to Dickens. They were apparently from a scrap supplier. The supplier did not exist; Lodge collected the cheques regularly from the accommodation address − in fact, a room over a shop − to which they were sent, and paid them into a bank account opened in the 'supplier's' name.

Lodge became concerned that the discrepancy between the amount of stock allegedly purchased and the amount actually on hand would become readily apparent. Victory began to make deliveries to Brighter of drums containing either worthless scrap or metals of a lower quality than that which they invoiced. In order to forestall any inquiries about invoices, Lodge sent a memo to accounting staff at Dickens asking them to process payments to Victory as a matter of urgency, in order to take advantage of a prompt payment discount.

Lodge had sole responsibility for keeping the stock records at Brighter Alloys. He told Dickens that he carried out a full stocktake every month and made sure that the stock records were accurate. Lodge's 'stocktakes' were only for show. He invented stock figures of his own that would ensure

Brighter Alloy's profits looked satisfactory. Occasionally Lodge would be asked about evident discrepancies between book stock and the goods at the warehouse. He would claim that these resulted from stock being in transit or at the firm's other site.

Brighter Alloy's auditors had traditionally accepted the stock figures supplied by the company. When new auditors Parker & Co. were appointed in 1987 by Dicken's new finance director they asked to attend stocktakes, but were deterred by Lodge, who claimed that he was too busy. He finally agreed − but he took care that the warehouse was arranged specially, with 'good' stock closest to the oxy-acetylene equipment needed to cut drums open. The oxy-acetylene pipe was deliberately shortened so that cutting equipment could not be used on the drums full of waste.

Lodge's downfall came in December 1988. Dicken's management was dissatisfied with Brighter Alloys' results, which had remained nearly static for the past few years. Peter Hart decided that the subsidiary should be sold off as soon as a buyer could be found. He insisted on a full stocktake as an aid to putting a value on the company. Hart suspected that Lodge was an inefficient manager − he blamed the company's poor results on this − and insisted on excluding him and his staff from taking part in the stock count. On the day of the count, Lodge was absent from work, claiming to be ill. He never returned to work. Within days of the stocktake, he was interviewed by the police in connection with the massive stock shortage which the stocktake had revealed. Lodge at first claimed that the company must have been burgled, but finally admitted his responsibility. He told police that the proceeds of his theft had been spent partly on his luxurious lifestyle, including a holiday home in Florida, performance cars and cabin cruiser, and partly on making good losses incurred by a business owned by his wife and son.

Lodge is due to be sentenced tomorrow.

14.4 Transcript of a meeting at the offices of Parker & Co., Bruddersford, on 31 March 1989

PRESENT: Walter Bell, senior partner (WB)
          John Lee, partner in charge of the Dickens audit (JL)
          Mark Clayton, manager on Dickens audit (MC)
          Barry Scott, audit senior on Dickens audit (BS)

WB As you know, John and I are due to meet the board of Dickens next week to discuss the whole business of the fraud at Brighter Alloys. They are extremely unhappy and embarrassed about the losses the group has suffered. Hart, in particular, is very upset, as he feels the affair has undermined his credibility, and he is clearly anxious to lay as much of the blame as possible on the auditors' shoulders. Now my view is that we did all that could reasonably be expected of us on the Brighter audit, and we have nothing to reproach ourselves with – but we do need to get the facts clear so that John and I are fully briefed for our meeting. I'd like to begin by sorting out the history of Brighter up to the time we were appointed. Can you start us off, John?

JL Yes, certainly. Brighter was founded in 1969 and its auditors were Slott & Co., who were a small firm then and remained that way. Brighter expanded dramatically, especially in the mid-1970s and early 1980s, but they kept Slott as auditors. Slott seem to have done little for them apart from providing an audit and preparing tax returns, but they had a good relationship with the management. The Dickens board occasionally made noises about the need to have the same auditors for the parent and all its subsidiaries, but they never did anything about it. When Hart came along, he forced the issue. He thought the group could achieve savings on the audit fee by having the same auditors throughout, and he was looking for a more positive attitude than Slott were displaying. He wanted suggestions about ways in which Brighter could tighten up its systems and improve performance.

WB What kind of audit work did Slott do?

MC I reviewed their files when we took over. They did a lot of vouching work, agreeing entries in the ledgers to purchase invoices and so on for months at a time. But they didn't do what we'd call a system audit. I suppose there wasn't much of a system to test, though. Certainly the work was carried out meticulously, and all the queries were followed up with Lodge. But it was very limited in scope, and the same programme was followed every year, even to testing the same months' transactions.

BS Well, they didn't attend the stocktake. That was always carried out by the managing director: originally Brightman, then Johnson, who took over when Dickens acquired them, then finally Lodge. The MD produced stock sheets, which they agreed to the trial balance and the balance sheet. And that was about all.

WB Did they ever make any comments in management letters?

JL I discussed this with the partner in Slott & Co. who looked after them. He said that if they had any problems, they always used to talk them over with Jack Brightman face to face, and they kept up that tradition with Johnson and then with Lodge. So they never put any comments in writing.

WB Mark, what were your impressions of Brighter when we took over the audit? I mean in terms of the way it was managed and run?

MC I knew that Hart wasn't happy about the efficiency of management, so I was expecting to see a shambles. In fact, I have to admit I was quite impressed with Lodge. He seemed to be on top of every aspect of the business – he had figures for debtors, bank balances, stock, everything, at his command. He was producing quarterly management accounts and monitoring performance. I could see that performance wasn't up to the targets Dickens had set, but it seemed to me that Lodge was working flat out to turn the company round. And he did work very hard; never took more than three or four days' holiday at a time and worked very long hours. He used to tell us about the place he had in Florida and how his wife went there on her own for holidays – he hadn't the time to go with her.

WB Didn't you find it odd that he had that, and ran a boat and various cars? The salary from Brighter wasn't all that good.

JL Mark and I discussed this once. We thought he did well – but he had told us about the shops his wife and son ran, and we assumed that those paid for the luxuries. And he'd had a high-powered job down south before he came here. He might have had savings from that.

WB Anyway, the first impression was that Lodge was making a fairly good job of running Brighter, but that division of duty was non-existent?

MC That's right. Barry can describe the way the office was run.

BS Basically, Lodge did all the key jobs himself. He didn't control the bank account; that was done centrally by Dickens. But he authorized all payments to suppliers and maintained the creditors ledger, so he could approve the addition of new suppliers. His secretary opened the mail and listed cheques; he did all the posting to the debtors ledger.

WB So how did this affect stock?

BS Lodge controlled stock all the way. The warehouse manager retired shortly after Lodge joined, and he was never replaced. Lodge claimed that it was a cost-cutting measure and that stock was so important that it needed the involvement of senior management. So the staff at the warehouse were basically labourers who weren't likely to venture to criticize what Lodge did.

WB   What was the stock system?

BS   The men at the warehouse kept delivery notes for goods received. When
     they made issues from stock, they made entries in a duplicate book. One
     copy of the page went with the goods; the other was sent to Lodge every
     week, along with that week's delivery notes. Lodge kept the stock records
     in his office and wrote them up about once a week; they were on lined
     cards with columns for receipts, issues and the balance.

     Lodge claimed to do a stocktake every month and to investigate any
     differences between the records and the actual amount on hand. He
     certainly walked round the warehouse, and he produced stock sheets ...

WB   But do we know whether they corresponded with the stock on hand?

MC   Short of attending a stocktake with him and checking all his figures, we
     couldn't tell.

WB   And we never did?

MC   We did ask on several occasions for a full stocktake when we were
     carrying out the 1987 audit. Lodge didn't want us to accompany him on
     the monthly stocktakes he did during the year. He said that it would
     have held him back too much if he had to explain everything as he went
     along. He could be very aggressive, and I suppose we didn't want to
     upset him at the start of our involvement with the company. If he had
     been unco-operative, it would have been disastrous, given that we were
     so heavily reliant on him for information and explanations in most of
     the audit areas.

WB   But you attended the year-end stocktake in 1987?

MC   One of our trainees attended part of it. It was very inconveniently timed.
     Lodge could manage to hold it only on Christmas Eve that year, because
     the company was going to close down until 6 January and Dickens
     needed to have figures on 3 January. Dickens agreed to the count being
     held on Christmas Eve because there weren't going to be any stock
     movements between then and the year-end. But Lodge started the count
     after lunch when most of our staff were off home for Christmas. I
     managed to find a junior trainee who lives locally who was prepared to
     attend.

WB   With any previous stocktaking experience?

MC   No, unfortunately. But he followed our standard procedures – made
     tests of some of Lodge's counts and took details of the stock sheets used.
     He found that the number of drums he counted agreed with Lodge's
     counts, and he had a few drums opened and ensured that they contained
     alloy and not scrap.

WB   What other audit work did we do on stock?

MC   This is a summary of the audit programme:

INTERIM TESTS

1. For a representative sample of 50 receipts per stock card:
 − check to delivery note and ensure details of quantity, type, etc. are in agreement;
 − agree price to supplier's invoice and check that total value on stock card has been correctly calculated.

2. For a representative sample of 50 issues from stock per stock card:
 − check to entry in duplicate book and ensure that details of quantity, type, etc. are in agreement;
 − ensure that amount issued has been deducted from the balance per the stock card.

3. For a representative sample of 50 stock cards, check accuracy of all additions and calculations.

4. Ensure that all journal adjustments to stock in excess of £25,000 have been authorized by Mr Lodge.

FINAL

1. Attend stocktake; perform test counts and complete report on attendance.

2. Check arithmetical accuracy of the stock sheets.

3. Trace totals from stock sheets to balance sheet.

4. Ensure that stocks are valued at invoice price on a FIFO basis, in accordance with company's policy.

5. Ensure by reference to current selling price list that stocks are valued at lower of cost and NRV.

6. Discuss with Mr Lodge the basis on which the obsolete stock provision has been calculated and ensure that it appears adequate.

WB And this is the audit work you carried out on stocks in 1987 and 1988?

JL Yes. Of course, we also included stocks in the company's and the group's letters of representation. Lodge signed the Brighter Alloys letter and Hart and the MD of Dickens signed for the group.

WB Did you find any errors in your testing?

JL No, nothing at all, really. The stock records seemed to be very accurately maintained and no errors emerged at the stocktake.

MC I can see that Dickens are upset, but surely they can't blame us for the loss, can they? We tested the accuracy of the records and they looked all right. We attended the stocktake; we ensured stock was valued in accordance with SSAP 9. I admit we missed the fraud, but any approach based on sampling involves a risk that errors will be overlooked. The audit isn't a guarantee that no fraud has occurred.

QUESTIONS FOR DISCUSSION

1. Mark comments that 'any approach based on sampling involves a risk that errors will be overlooked. The audit isn't a guarantee that no fraud has occurred'. How far do his views reflect the spirit of the auditing guidelines?
2. What measures might have prevented or detected the fraud at Brighter Alloys, and whose responsibility were they?

Relevant reading

Auditing Practices Committee (1990)
Woolf (1990), pp. 223–37, 411–23
Coopers & Lybrand (1985), pp. 42–63

Case 15
Banbury Group plc

BACKGROUND

Banbury Group plc (B) was founded as a private company in 1959 and went public in 1964. Its principal activities are the manufacture, sale and servicing of machinery for use in the food processing industry. Its year-end is 30 November.

DOCUMENTS

15.1 Summarized accounts of Banbury Group plc 1984–1986

£000	YEAR ENDED 30 NOVEMBER		
	1984	1985	1986
Turnover	27,849	41,508	39,320
Cost of sales	20,676	30,719	31,641
GROSS PROFIT	7,173	10,789	7,679
Selling and admin expenses	6,127	9,605	8,871
Other operating income	(256)	(138)	(347)
Redundancy costs	27	–	–
Interest receivable	(27)	(54)	(104)
Interest payable	645	1,235	1,229
PROFIT/(LOSS) BEFORE TAX	657	141	(1,970)
Total taxation	158	192	127
PROFIT/(LOSS) AFTER TAX	499	(51)	(2,097)
Minority interest	11	9	–
ATTRIBUTABLE TO MEMBERS	488	(60)	(2,097)
Extraordinary items	484	141	2,176
RETAINED PROFIT/(LOSS)	4	(201)	(4,273)

NOTES

Interest payable	1984	1985	1986
Short term	402	842	943
Long term	54	165	78
Debenture	–	52	51
Lease and HP	–	–	29
Other	189	176	128
	645	1,235	1,229

Profit before tax is after charging/(crediting):

	1984	1985	1986
Asset disposal	20	–	–
Subsidiary disposal	–	–	(186)
Grants received	(32)	(15)	–
Depreciation	484	660	795
Plant hire	166	253	318
Auditors' remuneration	99	166	175
Directors' emoluments	134	241	348
Compensation for loss of office	–	105	–

Staff costs:

Wages and salaries	7,188	11,118	8,590
Social security	1,196	1,915	2,697
Pensions	290	308	429
	8,674	13,341	11,716

Extraordinary items represent:

Merger costs	–	104	–
Reorganization expenses	263	88	–
Closure costs	221	–	–
Accelerated depreciation	–	–	382
Provision for costs of discontinuing business segment*	–	–	1,794
Taxation	–	(51)	–
	484	141	2,176

* The provision relates to the restructuring of production at Banbury Processing Equipment.

CONSOLIDATED BALANCE SHEETS

	1984	1985	1986
FIXED ASSETS			
Tangible fixed assets	4,494	4,997	5,193
Investments	17	17	21
	4,511	5,014	5,214
CURRENT ASSETS			
Stocks	6,572	10,180	10,457
Trade debtors	6,163	8,099	9,850
Other debtors	200	625	746
Prepayments	280	453	651
Tax recoverable	247	150	112
Cash	420	891	1,138
	13,882	20,398	22,954
CREDITORS (due within one year)			
Bank loans and overdrafts	2,526	5,022	6,293
Loans	195	437	768
Trade creditors	3,854	6,016	6,214
Bills of exchange	754	802	941
Current tax	28	34	105
Other taxes and social security	798	740	1,052
Other creditors	1,640	887	1,547
Accruals	2,016	2,974	2,557
	11,811	16,912	19,477
Net current assets	2,071	3,486	3,477
TOTAL ASSETS LESS CURRENT LIABILITIES	6,582	8,500	8,691
CREDITORS (due after one yea)			
Loans & debenture stock	1,375	2,715	3,222
Other creditors	275	353	662
PROVISIONS			
Other provisions	–	–	1,484
Deferred taxation	197	203	296
	1,847	3,271	5,664
	4,735	5,229	3,027

Capital	1,614	2,421	3,631
Share premium account	4,101	4,101	4,455
Merger reserve	–	597	699
Revaluation reserve	1,563	1,563	1,124
Profit & loss account	(2,562)	(3,503)	(6,901)
Minority interest	19	50	19
	4,735	5,229	3,027

STATEMENT OF SOURCE AND APPLICATION OF FUNDS

SOURCE OF FUNDS	1984	1985	1986
From operations	762	51	(1,253)
Asset disposal	140	204	637
Loans	174	347	1,207
Share issue	346	–	1,564
Tax repaid	–	–	101
	1,422	602	2,256

APPLICATION OF FUNDS			
Fixed assets	1,205	821	1,763
Taxation	252	135	–
Loan repayment	135	439	703
Minority interest	11	9	–
	1,603	1,404	2,466
	(181)	(802)	(210)

REPRESENTED BY			
Working capital			
Stocks	198	715	277
Debtors	1,038	970	2,070
Creditors	(788)	(1,261)	(1,202)
	448	424	1,145

Net liquid funds			
Cash	196	471	247
Bank loans/overdraft	(825)	(2,496)	(1,271)
Other loans	–	799	(331)
Increase (Decrease)	(629)	(1,226)	(1,355)
	(181)	(802)	(210)

15.2 Capital structure of Banbury Group plc

B's capital is made up of:

Ordinary shares of 10p	*28,244,674*	*£2,824,467*
Deferred ordinary shares of 10p	*8,069,907*	*£806,991*

15.3 Extract from permanent audit file: structure of Banbury Group plc

B is the parent company. The following are wholly owned subsidiaries:

Banbury Processing Equipment Ltd (incorporated in the UK)
Banbury North American Inc. (incorporated in USA)
Banbury France SA (incorporated in France)
Banbury BV (incorporated in The Netherlands)
Franklin Corporation Inc., incorporated in the USA, was acquired by B on 5 April 1985 and disposed of on 25 July 1987.

15.4 Chairman's statement at the annual general meeting of Banbury Group plc, held on 11 July 1987

The AGM approved the accounts for the year ended 30 November 1986. The Chairman stated:

1986 was an exceptionally difficult year for the group. The group's results were seriously affected by the substantial losses incurred both by Banbury Processing Equipment and by Franklin Corporation. The proceeds of the rights issue were mainly absorbed in paying the creditors of Banbury Processing Equipment, and not, as had been hoped, in reducing borrowings in order to stabilize the group's financial position. Your board concluded that the continuing programme of disposing of peripheral business segments was not by itself adequate to ensure that the group would return to financial stability. It concluded that it would be necessary to dispose of some of the core businesses so that the resources generated by disposal could be directed to those activities with the best prospects for the future. The group has accordingly undertaken a review of its activities, on the basis of which it has taken a number of significant decisions.

Banbury Processing Equipment is currently trading from two sites; the review we have undertaken suggests that this is not a viable basis for continuing operations. Accordingly, the company's plant at Reading is to be closed and the property disposed of during the current year. The group has entered into a contract with Stellar Properties to dispose of the site for £750,000 cash. The activities of the restructured company will be focused on currently profitable products and on products which have the potential to be made profitable. The order book is currently healthy, and a new managing director has recently joined the company. In order to improve the company's liquidity, the freehold interest in the company's site at Portsmouth is to be sold to Prospero Securities Ltd for a consideration of £1,550,000. The sale is subject to a lease-back to Banbury Processing Equipment for twenty-five years at an initial rent of £220,000, to be reviewed every five years.

The total employee numbers of the restructured company have been reduced from 450 at the end of 1986 to 199. The company is still constrained by a shortage of cash, but there are already implications that the restructured Banbury Processing Equipment is well placed to contribute to the future profitability of the group.

The benefits which the group had expected to arise from the merger with Franklin Corporation have not materialized. The profits which were confidently forecast at the time of the merger have not been achieved; instead, Franklin has suffered a substantial loss. This has been the result of technical problems experienced with new products which have had an adverse effect on sales. The US market has also shown a downturn, reflecting increased European competition. We have, unfortunately, no reason to expect that conditions will improve in the foreseeable future. Your board has accordingly taken the decision, subject to the approval of shareholders, to sell Franklin to Peoria Inc., for a consideration of £1,350,000.

The board is happy to report that the group's European subsidiaries have enjoyed a successful year. Banbury BV, in particular, has continued to develop markets in Germany, where the new products it introduced late in 1986 were well received. Both Banbury SA and Banbury BV have strong order books for the current year.

The restructuring described above will have the effect of reducing the group's borrowings by £5,900,000. The board is happy to record the group's gratitude to its principal bankers for their continuing support. In the UK, where cash constraints have been particularly acute, Barlloyds Bank has renewed the group's facility on normal terms, including the right to require repayment on demand, subject to the implementation of the restructuring programme and the continuing recovery of the group's financial position.

The group's trading loss and the provisions made for restructuring its operations have significantly eroded its reserves. As a result, the group has exceeded the borrowing limits imposed by its articles of association and by the 9% Debenture Stock 1989−96 Trust Deed. It is accordingly proposed that the group's borrowing limit be increased from one and one half to three and one half times its share capital and consolidated reserves. The trustee under the debenture stock deed has agreed to amend the trust deed, subject to an increase in the interest rate of the stock to 13 per cent with immediate effect.

[*Note*: The AGM ratified all the proposals contained in the Chairman's report.]

15.5   Interim report of Banbury Group plc for the half-year to 31 May 1987, issued 5 November 1987

(Comparative figures show six months ending 31 May 1986.)

£000	1987	1986
Sales	11,605	19,387
Operating costs	11,700	18,836
Interest payable	490	632
Loss before taxation	(585)	(81)
Taxation	36	103
Minority interest	–	2
Loss attributable to members	(621)	(186)
Extraordinary items*	(436)	–
Operating loss	(1,057)	(186)

* The extraordinary item represents the losses on disposal of Franklin Corporation.

The board wishes to report that the operating result was in line with expectations, although slightly affected by production delays at Portsmouth. It appears likely, however, that the shortfall will be made up by the end of the year. The asset disposal programme outlined in the Chairman's statement in August 1986 has been completed and the rationalization plan is being implemented. Interest charges for the first half-year have fallen substantially as a result of the disposal of Franklin Corporation and it is expected that the major reduction in borrowings in the UK will be reflected in a further interest reduction in the second half-year.

The continental subsidiaries continue to show satisfactory performance. Banbury BV is extending its factory in order to meet increasing demand for its products while reducing lead time for meeting orders. Banbury SA has experienced some production problems, but has launched a successful new product which is currently creating considerable interest. Banbury Processing Equipment continues to be the principal area of concern. Your board anticipates a gradual but steady improvement in the performance of the company rather than a spectacular recovery.

The group's net assets have now fallen below half the nominal value of its issued share capital. An Extraordinary General Meeting has been convened for 26 November to decide how the situation is to be dealt with.

15.6   Announcements by the board of Banbury Group plc

26 November 1987 At the Extraordinary General Meeting of Banbury Group plc held today, the Chairman stated that the board's initial intention, as outlined in its interim report, had been to continue with the restructuring plan approved at the AGM. It had become apparent, however, that the group would require further resources in order to carry out the planned restructuring. The group's strategy for obtaining additional finance was under discussion and a decision was to be expected in the next few weeks.

11 December 1987 The board is considering an approach made to it by Mr R. N. Bennett, Chief Executive of the group. This may result in an offer being made to buy its share capital. Various other third parties have expressed an interest in the group as a whole or in certain of its activities.

20 January 1988 At the request of the group, listing for its shares has been temporarily suspended with effect from 1.00 p.m. today.

13 February 1988 Following a deterioration in the group's financial position, the directors announce that the approach made by Mr R. N. Bennett has now been withdrawn. No progress has been made in discussions with the other parties who expressed an interest in the group.

In the absence of additional finance, the directors of Banbury Processing Equipment have decided that the company could not properly continue to trade. Barlloyds Bank was accordingly invited to appoint a receiver, and Messrs B. Smith and L. Simms of Parker and Simms were appointed joint administrative receivers of the company on 12 February 1988.

11 January 1989 At the request of the group, the listing for its securities suspended on 20 January 1988 has been cancelled with effect from 9.00 a.m. today.

QUESTIONS FOR DISCUSSION

The audit report on the Banbury Group's financial statements for the year ended 30 November 1986 was signed on 30 June 1987.

1. What aspects of the Banbury Group's results in 1986 might have given the auditor cause for concern? What work should the auditor have done in view of the circumstances of the Banbury Group?
2. On the basis of the evidence available to the auditor at the date when the audit report was signed, how should the audit report have been worded?

Relevant reading
Auditing Practices Committee (1989a):
  Auditing Guidelines: 4.410   The auditor's considerations in respect of going concern
Woolf (1990), pp. 616–22
Coopers & Lybrand (1985), pp. 462–75
Barnes and Hooi (1987)

Solution Notes

CASE 1   ALHAMBRA BINGO CLUBS

Subject matter

1. A new audit – ethical clearance; the engagement letter.
2. Planning a new audit – the sequence of testing; procedures for auditing branches.

Contents

Question 1 requires the student to set out the steps Gwynn & Co. must take at the beginning of the audit. First of all, they must contact Howells in writing and ask them whether there is any professional or other reason for the proposed change in auditor of which they should be aware in deciding whether or not to accept the appointment.

Assuming that there are no objections from Howells, Gwynn & Co. will now send an engagement letter to ABC, setting out the terms of their engagement. It will be necessary to adapt the terms of the letter to fit the circumstances of this appointment. In particular:

1. Howells appear to have carried out the year-end stocktakes and cash counts themselves. This is not part of the auditor's responsibilities. If Gwynn & Co. intend to do this work, they should specify that it is being provided as an 'other service'. If they do not intend to do it – and in view of their staffing problems at the year-end it will not be a priority – the letter should refer to this, to avoid any misunderstanding.
2. The letter should mention the provision of accounting and tax services – the preparation of the financial statements and corporation tax return – as requested by Simon.
3. The provision of systems advice – in particular about the purchase of a computer – should be mentioned under 'other services'.
4. PF comments in Document 1.5 that Howells spent several weeks checking the club returns. This level of substantive testing should not be necessary unless ABC's system contains fundamental weaknesses, and prima facie Gwynn & Co. should not plan to repeat it this year. ABC may, however, expect this level of testing. Management may possibly expect the auditors to comment on, say, the quality of reporting by individual club managers. Gwynn & Co. should, therefore, emphasize in the letter that they will carry out selective testing only unless circumstances require in-depth testing. If ABC wish Gwynn & Co. to perform tests on the club returns as, in effect, an internal audit procedure, this should be stated in the letter.

5. The arrangements for charging and billing ABC for the different audit and non-audit services to be provided should be made clear.

Question 2:

(a) Given that the firm will be short-staffed in June, and that in any case the accounts must be completed by 1 July, an interim audit is clearly needed to cover as much ground as possible before the year-end. Gwynn & Co. should aim to start this promptly, as they will need to spend some time documenting the systems in detail and possibly doing walk-through tests before beginning the systems tests proper. It seems advisable for club visits to take place at the interim stage, for the reasons noted below.

(b) The bulk of the work will have to be done at ABC's head office in Cardiff, where the accounts staff are based and most of the records are kept. In view of the amount of input provided by the club managers, however, the auditors will also need to visit some of the clubs. Visiting all the clubs this year would be extremely time-consuming and would probably not provide enough additional evidence to be justified, but consideration might well be given to setting up a rotational programme of visits, so that all the clubs are visited, say, every three years and the major ones in terms of turnover − or any which give special cause for concern − are visited more often.

   This year, for instance, the auditors might visit Cardiff, Swansea and Port Talbot as the biggest clubs, possibly Neath, which shows a rather low return on turnover, and one or two others. Discussions with management might help to identify suitable cases.

   There seems to be no justification for counting cash and taking stock − or attending these operations − at all clubs, as the amounts involved are individually immaterial.

(c) Areas for particular attention here might include:

   (i) *Club turnover* Ensure that sequential controls over cards issued are being operated by testing the completeness of the sequences in the returns made to head office (to ensure that undeclared sales are not being made).

      Trace bingo, gaming machine and café takings from club summaries to the nominal ledger and vice versa.

      Analytically review turnover and margin by activity and by club to ensure that any fluctuations can be adequately explained.

   (ii) *Cash and bank* Trace bankings per bank statement to paying-in slips and to club cash takings records and vice-versa, to ensure that takings are banked promptly and completely.

      Analytically review levels of month-end cash and petty cash purchases by branch and investigate fluctuations.

   (iii) *Purchases* In view of the difficulties encountered last year, it may be advisable to circulate major suppliers at the interim audit and reconcile balances reported with those in the purchase ledger. This should give some indication of possible problem accounts for follow-up, and interim balances confirmed can be rolled forward to the year-end.

(iv) *Fixed assets* Inspection of freehold title deeds and of additions at Swansea (to be visited anyway) should be adequate.

(v) *Stock* As noted above, 100 per cent stocktake attendance is unnecessary, but consideration should be given to attending one or two counts, mainly to ensure that procedures (which form part of the monthly routine) are satisfactory.

Analytical review of monthly stock levels throughout the year should be used to alert the auditor to any problem branches.

(vi) *Club visits* These should include observation of stock and cash counts (not necessarily the year-end ones) and of the procedures for controlling the issue and recording of card sales. Banking procedures should also be noted, to ensure they comply with head office's instructions.

The club visit also gives an opportunity for the auditor to observe procedures in action and note any shortcomings, for instance in physical security, which may influence the degree of assurance placed on information received from clubs.

(d) Delays by clubs in submitting purchase invoices received may pose a problem, particularly as there is so little time between the year-end and the date for reporting to the bank. As well as circularizing creditors, Gwynn & Co. might consider a close review of branch profitability in May, to ensure that any unusually high margins do not indicate unreported liabilities.

Some of the client's comments hint at problems in obtaining reports from club managers. The auditors will have to assess the reliability of club reports at an early stage as any shortcomings will result in a need for increased substantive testing.

CASE 2   ELLIOTT TRANSMITTERS PLC

Subject matter

The case requires students to identify key controls and weaknesses in a sales system, using information which includes flowcharts and systems notes. They are also required to produce a flowchart, based on the notes of a conversation describing the system in question.

Contents

The first question requires students to flowchart the system for taking and accepting customer orders. This is mainly described in the interview with the sales manager; a suggested solution is given opposite. Narrative notes will probably be needed to indicate the nature of the checks carried out before the order can be approved. It should be noted that the second and third copies of the order confirmation are sent outside the sales order department, going respectively to the despatch department and the sales ledger department. In a 'real' flowchart, they would be referenced to the pages dealing with the despatch and sales ledger systems. Copy 2 does, in fact, appear on the relevant page of the flowchart shown in Document 2.5.

The narrative notes referred to above, which would form part of the flowchart, might take the following form.

Creditworthiness checks (flowchart ref. 5)

1. Existing customers
On receipt of an order from an existing customer, the following procedures are adopted:
(a) value of sales order checked with sales ledger balance and credit limit;
(b) if credit clearance approved, customer account number is entered on to order;
(c) if credit limit exceeded, the documentation is checked by the sales manager, who either:
  (i) approves the order, in which case the customer account number is entered on the order; or
  (ii) rejects the order, in which case he contacts the customer and sends a rejection letter. The sales order, customer order and rejection letter are filed together alphabetically.

2. New customers
On receipt of an order from a new customer, the following procedures are followed:
(a) credit rating agency requested to supply credit reference (letter A);
(b) if credit clearance approved (letter B), the sales manager enters customer details, account number and credit limit on the sales ledger master file amendment form; the account number is entered on the order;
(c) if credit clearance is rejected, a rejection letter is sent to the customer, requesting payment in advance (letter C);
(d) filing arrangements:
  Letter A − in sales order department, alphabetically;
  Letter B − in sales order department, alphabetically with letter A;
  Letter C − in sales order department, alphabetically with sales order and customer order.

3. Review of credit limits
There is no formal system for regular review of credit limits, although they are occasionally revised by the sales manager on an *ad hoc* basis.

ELLIOTT TRANSMITTERS
Procedures for taking customer order

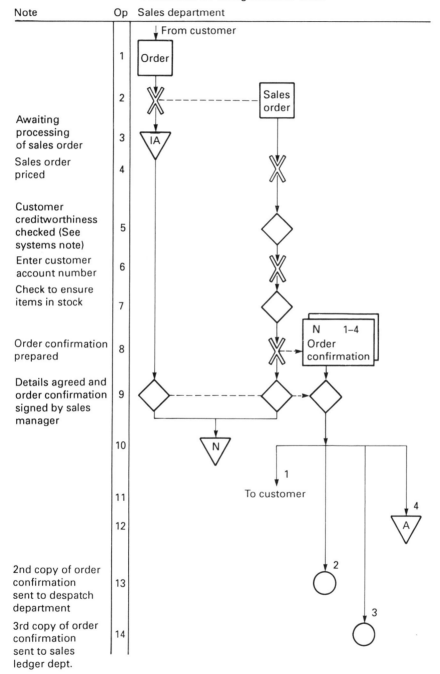

Note	Op	Sales department
		From customer
	1	Order
	2	Sales order
Awaiting processing of sales order	3	IA
Sales order priced	4	
Customer creditworthiness checked (See systems note)	5	
Enter customer account number	6	
Check to ensure items in stock	7	
Order confirmation prepared	8	N 1–4 Order confirmation
Details agreed and order confirmation signed by sales manager	9	
	10	N
	11	To customer
	12	A
2nd copy of order confirmation sent to despatch department	13	
3rd copy of order confirmation sent to sales ledger dept.	14	

The second question requires students to identify key controls and weaknesses within the accounting system. This requires the student to identify the steps that will be needed to ensure that a specific control objective is met, and to determine whether ET's controls are adequate. The key control objectives and the relevant controls or weaknesses in ET's system are listed below.

1. *Customer orders require approval of credit and terms before acceptance.* The system requires credit references to be obtained before a new customer is taken on, and also requires that references are checked before an existing customer is sent more goods. It does not, however, require that credit limits are reviewed. This presents the risk that goods will be sent to a customer whose creditworthiness had deteriorated since originally having been accepted by ET. As a result, there is a possibility that the control objective will not be achieved.

2. *Uncollectable amounts are promptly identified and provided for.* Uncollectable amounts will tend to be older balances. It is reasonable to conclude that the older the balance, the more likely it is that the debtor will not pay. As a result, it is important that credit control staff should have reliable information about the age of debtors. The system produces an aged analysis, but there are no controls to ensure that the ageing is correct. (Such controls might include a review by a member of the sales ledger department or a built-in computer check.) As a result, it would be possible for an error to go undetected for some time, and hence for ET to fail to provide for an irrecoverable bad debt.

3. *Goods despatched or services rendered are invoiced.* The system includes a number of relevant controls:
   (a) As shown on the flowchart, the gatekeeper compares the goods being despatched with those shown on the despatch note. This ensures that the despatch note is an accurate reflection of the goods that have been sent to a customer.
   (b) There is also a check that all the fourth copies of the despatch note processed by the sales ledger department are input to the computer, and hence that they finally generate an invoice. (This is achieved by the use of hash totals, which are checked both manually and by the computer.)
   However, there is no check that all despatch notes raised result in invoices. For instance, if the fourth copy of a despatch note were lost on its way to the sales ledger department, no sales invoice would be raised, and nothing would alert the accounts staff to the oversight. It would be possible to rectify this defect in the system fairly easily. If the sales ledger department regularly check the numerical sequence of the despatch notes, which are returned there after processing, it would be able to identify despatch notes which were missing from the sequence. It would then be possible to use another copy of the despatch note (e.g. that filed in despatch department) to produce the invoice.

The absence of such a control could result in failure to invoice deliveries; the fact that ET has suffered a large drop in gross profit margin suggests the same problem. This drop in margin is tentatively explained as a stock loss. If deliveries were not being invoiced, the stock figure derived from the physical stocktake would reflect the movement of stock, but the sales figure would be understated — hence the decline in gross margin.

4. *Invoices are for the correct amount.* For the invoice amount to be correct, it is necessary that both the quantity and the price are correctly input.

The batch control procedure includes a hash total based on the quantities in the despatch notes; this should prevent misstatement of quantities in invoices.

The agreement of the prices on the sales master file to the current sales price list should prevent the use of incorrect prices in calculating invoices.

In addition, the sales ledger clerk checks the correctness of the invoice casts and calculations.

5. *Sales are recorded correctly as to account, amount and period.* The nominal ledger control account is reconciled to the list of balances monthly. This reconciliation is reviewed by the chief accountant. The control account reconciliation is a check that sales are correctly recorded in respect of amount and period; any misposting would show up as a reconciling item.

The sales day book totals are agreed to the hash totals by the data control clerk. The hash totals include a hash total of customer account numbers. This should ensure that sales are posted to the correct customer account.

6. *Recorded invoices are for valid transactions.* The matching of invoices with despatch notes is a relevant control here. However, the extent of this matching is not clear from the systems notes. If, for instance, the matching checked only that the customer invoiced was the one who had received the delivery, it would be possible for errors to be made — e.g. invoicing for the wrong amount or type of goods.

The more important control is the use of hash totals which are checked to the sales ledger print-out. This ensures that all features of the invoice — customer, quantity of goods and type of goods — are in agreement with the despatch note.

The gatekeeper checks goods despatched against the despatch sheet and load sheet. This control ensures that the despatch note is an accurate record of the goods which have been sent to customers.

The third question requires students to devise tests which are responsive to the controls and weaknesses noted in Question 2. The extent of testing required will vary, depending on the amount of reliance which it is considered can be placed on the controls. Suggested tests are as follows.

Customer orders require approval of credit and terms before acceptance

The failure to review credit limits means that there is a risk that large debts will prove uncollectable. The system does not include any controls which compensate for this weakness. Hence, there is no point in carrying out tests on the system for approving orders; the overriding weakness means that the auditor cannot rely on the system. Instead, there is a need to carry out substantive testing to ensure that balances at the year-end are collectable. Such tests might include:

1. circularization of large and/or old balances;
2. comparison of year-end balances, especially large/old ones, with cash received after the year-end;
3. review of the conduct of large/old balances to ensure that it does not indicate a deterioration in the customer's credit status, e.g. increasing overdue balance, increasing delay in making payments.

The tests suggested above are, however, dependent on the accuracy of the ageing of debts. It has been noted that there is no control to ensure that the aged analysis is correctly compiled. This is considered in the next section.

Uncollectable amounts are promptly identified and provided for

Unless the sales ledger is correctly aged, uncollectable balances will not be identified. As no control exists over the accuracy of ageing, it will be necessary to test this substantively. This might be done by:

1. testing the ageing of a number of balances to ensure that it has been correctly carried out, i.e. that invoices have been assigned to the correct period and that cash payments are being correctly applied to the invoices to which they relate;
2. circularizing a sample of debtor balances, including large balances, in order to gain assurance that material balances are recoverable;
3. comparing year-end debtor balances with cash received after the year-end: situations where later invoices have apparently been paid before earlier ones should be investigated, as they may reveal either mistakes in ageing or amounts which are in dispute and hence likely to be uncollectable;
4. comparing the bad debt provision with:
   (a) total debtor balances;
   (b) debts that are more than ninety days old,
      in both 1989 and 1988 to ensure that ET is following similar policies in the two years and that the 1989 provision is reasonable in the light of what is known about debtors.

These tests will attack the problem in two ways: they will provide evidence as to the correctness of ageing and also give comfort as to the collectability of year-end balances.

Goods despatched or services rendered are invoiced

Here, again, there is a fundamental weakness in the system. As noted above, there is no sequence check to ensure that all despatch notes have resulted in the production of an invoice. The existence of stock losses and fluctuating gross margins also suggests that some despatches are not being invoiced. There appears to be a high risk of material error, and the auditor should be put on alert to design tests accordingly. These tests might include:

1. Considering the possibility that other controls exist which may compensate for the lack of sequence control. For instance, the order confirmation is kept on temporary file in the despatch department until the despatch note has been raised. If the despatch department regularly reviews the temporary file and follows up old outstanding items, some uninvoiced deliveries would be noted. If such a control exists, its operation should be tested.
2. In the absence of any such compensating control, the auditor may find it necessary to carry out a sequence test on the year's despatch notes filed in the sales ledger department, and ensure that all numbers in the sequence were accounted for. Any missing numbers should be investigated, to ensure that there was a valid reason for their absence, such as destruction of a note raised in error. It is recognized that follow-up of missing items may be time consuming, but it appears desirable, given the risk of material error.

Invoices are for the correct amount

The three controls noted above can be tested here.

1. Check that the sales price master file print-out has been compared by the sales manager with the approved price list. It will be necessary to check both that the comparison is performed, and that it represents a bona fide check, i.e. that the sales manager notices and corrects errors. To do this, it might be advisable to test a number of prices on one print-out, to ensure that they correspond with those on the price list, and then check other lists for evidence of manager review, e.g. ticks or a signature.
2. Check that the sales ledger clerk checks casts and calculations. Here again, this might take the form of re-performance on a number of items, to ensure that the clerk's work is accurate, followed by a review to check that the clerk is testing all items, e.g. by marking invoices as checked.
3. Test the control over hash totals, to ensure that:
   (a) hash totals of part numbers and quantities are correctly calculated;
   (b) hash totals are checked to the sales day book after processing and any differences investigated.

Sales are recorded correctly as to account, amount and period

1. The nominal ledger control account reconciliation should be checked, to ensure that it is carried out regularly and accurately. This could be done by checking one reconciliation in detail and following up reconciling items and then reviewing the other reconciliations to ensure that one had been performed for each month of the year.
2. The use of the hash total of customer account numbers as a control should be tested:
   (a) by checking the calculation of the account number hash total for a batch of despatch notes;
   (b) by testing the procedure for comparing hash totals with the sales day book print-out.

Recorded invoices are for valid transactions

1. Here again, the use of hash totals — of quantities, part numbers and customer account numbers — act as a control to ensure that invoice details are in agreement with despatch notes and hence that invoices represent valid transactions.
2. The gatekeeper's check of despatch sheets and goods is a control which should prevent incorrect despatch notes and hence incorrect invoices. This is not a control which can readily be tested by sampling, as it would be impracticable to attempt observation over a number of days. It would, however, be possible to observe the procedure on one occasion, to ascertain whether the gatekeeper appears to be carrying out the check carefully and accurately, and to discuss with the gatekeeper how he does the work and how he deals with any problems, such as finding loads which do not correspond to the despatch note.
3. As noted earlier, this case does not deal with ET's system for handling credits. It might be noted, however, that a review of credit notes given to customers would also highlight the existence of invoicing errors if it indicated that customers were being given credits in respect of invoices issued for which no goods had been received.

It should be noted that, once the auditor has identified those tests which are relevant to a particular control objective, it is possible to consider whether tests can be combined, or whether one test will relate to more than one objective. This is the case here. For instance, a single debtors circularization can cover the first and second objectives described above provided that the sample includes all the types of balances which need to be tested. Similarly, the tests on cash totals could be combined. In this way, it will be possible to reduce repetition of work and to ensure that a single test covers as much ground as possible.

CASE 3   GREEN FINGERS LIMITED

Subject matter

This case deals with the audit problems presented by a small company with little segregation of duties. It can be contrasted with Elliott Transmitters (Case 2), where there is a high degree of segregation of duties and numerous controls are in place to ensure correct processing of transactions.

Contents

The first question requires students to identify possible problem areas for the auditor of a small company. This is a topic which has received relatively little attention in the literature, although there has recently been considerable debate about the retention or abolition of the small company audit. The main problem faced by the small company auditor is often the absence of internal controls. Small companies will normally have only a small accounts department and staff will often be unqualified. There will be little or no segregation of duties, for two reasons. The small size of the department will mean that there are not enough people available to split duties for control purposes; for instance, one person may be involved in both credit control and cashier functions. In addition, it will be necessary for staff to be involved in all aspects of the business in order to provide cover in case of absence or to help at busy times. The resulting organization will be very different from that at Elliott Transmitters (Case 2), where staff duties were quite rigorously segregated.

The absence of segregation of duties does not of itself mean that the small company's accounts will not give a true and fair view, but it does mean that the auditor will have to consider the existence of other controls and the use of strategies other than systems testing. One major control in the small company will often be the close involvement of directors in the day-to-day running of the business. This is a good safeguard against misstatement and error by staff, as the directors' close involvement may deter attempts at fraud and should mean that the accounting function is being performed by people with a good understanding of the needs of the business. To that extent, it could be argued that small companies with able and active directors may have more effective accounting systems than large companies that rely on junior staff with little understanding of the business as a whole. The close involvement of directors does, however, also create potential problems. In particular, it would be possible for a director to use his or her authority to override controls in the system; employees would find it difficult to prevent this from happening.

Thus, the auditor cannot automatically regard the close involvement of directors in the business as an assurance that the accounting system is satisfactory. He or she will need to consider what tasks the director carries out, but this must be supplemented by audit testing, involving systems tests,

substantive tests and analytical review, in order to gain assurance that the
system is performing satisfactorily.

Similarly, the auditor may often find that management explanations and
assurances are the only available source of audit evidence, for instance as to
the reason for a particular trend in profits or the recoverability of a debt.
The auditor would not be performing his or her duty in accepting such
assurances at face value; he or she should consider whether management
assurances are consistent with other audit evidence, and also how reliable
they have proved in the past, before using them as a basis for a conclusion.
It will not, therefore be possible for the auditor to gain assurance on a
particular issue simply by ensuring that it is covered by the letter of representation, although the letter of representation may be used as an adjunct
to audit tests.

Another problem posed by the small company for the auditor is that of
carrying out an audit at a cost which will be acceptable to the client.
Substantive testing will tend to be more time consuming and labour-intensive
than systems testing, which will increase the cost of auditing a small
company relative to that of a larger one with more developed systems. The
auditor will need to exercise judgement in devising the most cost-effective
audit plan.

The points made above should not be taken to imply that the small
company with few systems is unauditable. It should be possible to gain
sufficient audit evidence to report on the small company's accounts, but the
audit approach to the smaller company will tend to be different from the
audit of large companies.

The second question requires the student to identify key controls in
the purchases, payroll, stock and fixed assets systems. The question then
requires this information to be used in devising audit tests of these systems.
Suggested controls and tests are as follows.

Purchases and creditors

1. Expenditure on goods and services is made only with proper authorization.
2. Goods, services, expenses, fixed assets and related liabilities are recorded
   correctly as to account, amount and period.

Controls
(a) Mr Clayton authorizes all expenditure on goods or services.
(b) The accounts clerk matches the goods received note (GRN), purchase
    order and invoice before recording the purchase.
(c) The assistant accounts clerk checks invoice additions, extensions and
    pricing.
(d) The accountant reviews the nominal ledger coding.

Tests
(a) Discuss with accounts clerk and observe, the procedures adopted for:
  (i) matching GRN, purchase order and invoice;
  (ii) checking arithmetical accuracy of invoice;
  (iii) reconciling supplier statements.
(b) Discuss with accountant, and observe, his procedures for reviewing nominal ledger codings, reconciliation and analytical review.
(c) Discuss with Mr Clayton, and observe, his procedures for approving expenditure.
(d) Select a representative sample of twenty-five purchase invoices on a random basis and:
  (i) agree details to GRN;
  (ii) check arithmetical accuracy of invoice;
  (iii) ensure nominal ledger coding appears reasonable;
  (iv) agree details to purchase day book;
  (v) agree posting to purchase ledger account.
(e) Check arithmetical accuracy of purchase day book and its posting to nominal ledger for two months of the year.
(f) Vouch all fixed asset additions over £1,000 to invoices.
(g) Review year-end purchase ledger reconciliation in detail and obtain explanations for all reconciling items. Test the extraction of the list of balances from the purchase ledger.
(h) For all purchase ledger invoices over £500 for two weeks before and after the year-end, check accuracy of inclusion in the stock records and purchase day book.
(i) Obtain the client's list of accruals and prepayments. Vouch all items exceeding £500 to supporting documentation.
(j) Agree or reconcile all purchase ledger balances over £500 at the year-end, plus a representative sample of twenty-five others, to supplier statements.
(k) Review cash book payments and invoices received after the year-end. Ensure all items exceeding £500 have been accrued for if necessary.
(l) Review monthly analysis of gross margins. Obtain explanation for any significant fluctuations.
(m) Compare:
  (i) trading account expenses;
  (ii) accruals and prepayments;
  with previous period and obtain explanations for any significant fluctuations.

Comments
Note how the audit tests combine substantive testing, systems testing and analytical review. Mr Clayton's involvement is prima facie taken as a control, but the auditor is also seeking to confirm the strength of control by obtaining independent evidence of creditor balances (via supplier statement reconciliation) and reviewing results to ensure that they are reasonable.

Payroll

3. Salaries, wages and related costs are incurred only for work authorized and performed.
4. Salaries, wages and related costs are calculated at the proper rate.
5. Salaries, wages, related costs and liabilities are recorded correctly as to account, amount and period.

Controls
(a) The accountant approves time sheets and payroll amendments including starters and leavers, rates of pay and bonuses.
(b) Mr Clayton checks the clerical accuracy of the payroll and reviews it for unusual items.

Tests
(a) Discuss with Mr Clayton, and observe, his procedures for checking and reviewing the payroll.
(b) Discuss with the accountant, and observe, his procedures for approving payroll amendments and time sheets.
(c) Perform an analytical review of the payroll expense for each month of the year, with reference to employee numbers, pay rates, overtime worked, holidays and any other factors likely to influence the payroll expense. Ensure that the results appear reasonable in the light of influencing factors. Obtain explanations for any unexpected fluctuations.
(d) Calculate payroll accrual by reference to the payroll payments after the year-end.
(e) Calculate the PAYE/NI accrual at the year-end and agree or reconcile to the amounts subsequently paid out.

Comments
Analytical review is suggested as the principal test here because it is likely to be less time consuming than systems testing. If the monthly payroll figure appears reasonable in the light of what is known about the numbers employed and the prevailing rates of pay, the auditor can reasonably conclude that the payroll expense is fairly stated.

Stocks and work in progress

6. Costs are assigned to stock and work in progress at year-end in accordance with the stated valuation method.
7. Stock and work in progress quantities are accurately recorded and extended.
8. Physical loss of stock is prevented or promptly detected.
9. Obsolete, slow-moving and excess stock is prevented or promptly detected and provided for.
10. Stock and work in progress are carried at the lower of cost and net realizable value.

Controls
(a) The accountant investigates differences between physical counts and the stock records.
(b) Mr Clayton approves all adjustments to the stock records.
(c) Mr Clayton performs a daily review of all stock records.

Tests
(a) Discuss with Mr Clayton and the accountant the procedure for comparing book and physical stock, investigating differences and authorizing stock adjustments.
(b) Attend the year-end stocktake. Select a sample of stock items, to include all with a book value in excess of £500 and a representative sample of twenty-five others, and perform test counts of them. Record the details of documents showing the last movements of items to and from the premises for subsequent cut-off testing.
(c) Trace test-counts to final stocksheets. Test-check the accuracy of additions and calculations of stock sheets and trace totals to balance sheet.
(d) For a representative sample, as outlined in (b) above, test-check prices on stock sheets to stock cards and invoices, ensuring that items have been valued on a FIFO basis.
(e) Review valuation of growing crops to ensure that quantity estimated by Mr Clayton appears reasonable and valuation approximates to cost.
(f) Ensure that cut-off has been carried out correctly by:
    (i) following up cut-off information obtained at the stocktake to ensure it has been dealt with in the correct period;
    (ii) reviewing purchase and sales day books for two weeks before and two weeks after the year-end and checking that stock purchases or sales exceeding £500 have been accounted for in the correct period.
(g) Agree stock figures to the balance sheet and notes to the accounts. Check that they have been valued in accordance with GF's stated accounting policy and in compliance with SSAP 9.
(h) Discuss with the nursery manager and Mr Clayton the existence of obsolete, slow-moving and excess stock. Ensure that, if such stock exists, adjustment has been made to write it down to net realizable value.
(i) Review sales of growing crops post year-end and ensure they have been sold at more than cost.

Comments
It will not be possible for the auditor to obtain direct confirmation that the quantity of growing crops is correctly stated. This is an area where the auditor will need to make use of the figure supplied by management, confirmed via the letter of representation; it can be corroborated by the auditor's own judgement and by the results of other tests, e.g. analytical review of gross margins.

Property, plant and equipment

11. Disposal and scrapping of plant are identified and recorded correctly as to account, amount and period.
12. Physical loss of property, plant and equipment is prevented.
13. Depreciation is calculated using proper lives and methods.

Controls
(a) All disposals are authorized by Mr Clayton.
(b) Mr Clayton maintains the fixed asset register and reconciles it annually to the nominal ledger.
(c) Mr Clayton checks the accuracy of the depreciation calculation.

Tests
(a) Inquire of Mr Clayton the procedure for reviewing and approving depreciation calculations and disposals.
(b) Perform a detailed analytical review of the depreciation charge, taking into account additions, asset lives and depreciation policy. Compare the charge with the previous period and obtain an explanation for any unexpected fluctuations.
(c) Reconcile the fixed asset register with the nominal ledger.
(d) Confirm with Mr Clayton whether any fixed asset disposals took place during the year. If there were any, vouch them to supporting documentation and check the calculation of the gain or loss on disposal.

Comments
Here again, analytical review offers an opportunity to obtain audit comfort on a major expense without time-consuming detailed testing.

This suggested programme is a very comprehensive one and students may well have overlooked certain tests or may have different ones to suggest. The key point that it should convey is the importance of combining three kinds of tests − systems testing, substantive testing and analytical review − in order to achieve the most efficient audit coverage.

CASE 4   ESPARTO LIMITED

Subject matter

The case presents students with management accounting information and requires them to perform an analytical review of it in order to identify potential areas of audit risk. (This can be contrasted with the case of Holiday Holdings (Case 12), where analytical review is to be used as a direct test of balances.)

Contents

The first question requires the student to identify those items which could indicate problem areas on the audit. The following are suggested as indicators of possible problems.

1. Stock levels have fallen very markedly since last year-end. They are currently 36 per cent down on 1988 (£280,000 as against £441,000) and 12.5 per cent down on budget. This could indicate a deliberate stock reduction policy, introduced after the budget was finalized; possibly the difference between the March 1988 and December 1988 figures reflects seasonal factors. There is a possibility, however, that stock is misstated, and that this has caused the apparent drop in the stock figure. This observation is nothing like conclusive evidence, but it should alert the auditor to the possibility of misstatement and remind him or her to direct testing towards the detection of stock understatement, e.g. by test-counts from physical stock to book stock.

2. The average debt collection period has increased perceptibly – from just under forty-two days in 1988 to nearly forty-four days. This increase was not budgeted for. This could indicate a general slight slowing-down in the speed at which E's debtors are paying up. Alternatively, it might be caused by one or two large debtors who are delaying payment, because of a dispute or because of financial difficulties. The auditor will need to investigate further in order to explain this trend.

3. The return on capital employed (ROCE) has deteriorated sharply, both against previous actual figures and against budget. This year's result is less than half that achieved in 1988. A number of factors may be implicated in this. Fixed assets have increased since last year; as noted by the managing director, E is undertaking a programme of improvements to its plant. ROCE might be expected to drop slightly until the plant improvements start to pay for themselves through increased efficiency and higher sales.

   A second factor affecting ROCE is the poor sales performance. Actual sales to December 1988 are £2,952,000 against a budgeted £3,115,000. At this rate, unless performance improves substantially in the final quarter, E's 1989 result will be slightly down on 1988, rather than achieving the 5 per cent growth which the managing director mentioned as a continuing target. It is too early to speak of going concern problems in a company which has reserves and is trading profitably. It should be borne in mind, however, that the management of a subsidiary which is underperforming may feel pressure from head office to improve results. Management attitudes at E to such issues as stock valuation or bad debt provision may be coloured by the wish to produce the best possible profit figures under the circumstances.

4. Selling and administration expenses have declined in relation to sales volume. They were £563,000 in the year ended 31 March 1988 in relation

to sales of £3,949,000 – i.e. 14.3 per cent of sales. In the period to December 1988 they have dropped to 11.8 per cent of sales (348/2,952). This could reflect a reduction in the sales force; but this would be a surprising step for E's management to take in view of its avowed intention to push hard for increased sales. Is there some misstatement of overheads – particularly in the areas of advertising, marketing and commission – which has led to this unexpected result? Some further audit investigation seems to be necessary.

5. Contribution is falling as a percentage of sales. In 1987 it was 52 per cent, in 1988, 50 per cent and for the period to December 1988 it has dropped to 48 per cent. In this period, direct materials accounted for 85 per cent of direct costs, compared with 72 per cent in 1987 and 78 per cent in 1988. There are a number of possible explanations for this. It may be that materials prices are rising faster than labour costs, e.g. because of an unfavourable exchange rate trend. Alternatively, labour costs may be falling proportionately because improved plant has enabled E to make more efficient use of labour. A further possibility, however, is that the apparent increase in materials costs reflects problems within E. Difficulties with the new plant might result in increased wastage of materials; there might be stock losses through inefficient stock systems, theft or damage, which are reflected in an increased cost of materials.

The use of analytical review at the planning stage of an audit has to be circumspect. Observations made at this stage should be used to suggest questions which the auditor needs to ask; they cannot in themselves be conclusive audit evidence. The use of analytical review findings as a basis for determining what questions to ask is dealt with further in the second discussion question.

Taking the various components of the financial statements one by one, the auditor might pose the following questions.

Balance sheet

Fixed assets
1. What are the fixed asset improvements?
2. What is the 1989 budget for capital expenditure?
3. What disposals have taken place?
4. What is E's depreciation policy, in terms of rates used, method, commencement and cessation of depreciation?

Stock
1. Why has stock declined since last year?
2. Why are stock levels significantly below budget?
3. Why has the budgeted figure been set below that for last year?
4. Is the stock level liable to seasonal fluctuations?
5. Has the purchasing system changed (e.g. to a just-in-time approach, which might result in lower stockholdings)?

6. Have costs per unit of raw materials fallen since last year?
7. Does the lower stock figure reflect a price reduction, a quantity reduction or both?

Debtors
1. The average collection period was budgeted to remain unchanged from 1988. It has increased by two days. Debtors turnover has declined by more than the budgeted decrease. Is there any reason for these changes?
2. What are the credit terms E offers to customers?
3. Have these terms changed in any way?
4. Can we analyse the debtors ledger so as to identify the major accounts and see how these have moved since last year?
5. Does E make any cash sales? If so, who are its cash customers?
6. What is E's discount policy?
7. What is the level of returns by customers?
8. What is the level of credit notes given (in respect of returned goods, damaged goods etc.)?
9. Have the levels of returns and credit notes changed since last year?
10. Have there been any production problems which could have affected product quality and hence led to disputes with customers?

Due from subsidiaries
1. What is the nature of E's trade with other Parchment group companies?
2. On what terms do subsidiaries trade with one another?
3. How readily are these balances collectable?
4. How often do subsidiaries settle their accounts?

Cash/overdraft
Cash balances are below budget. The cash position has worsened since 1987. Why has this occurred?

Financial leases
1. What items are leased?
2. Over what periods are assets leased?
3. Are leased assets depreciated on the same basis as purchased ones?

Creditors
1. Average payment periods have decreased by more than budget even though the budget figure was worse than in previous years. Why is this the case?
2. Can we analyse the creditors ledger to identify the major accounts and see how they have moved since last year?
3. How many major suppliers are there? (Reliance on too few can lead to production problems.)
4. What are the credit terms offered by major suppliers? Is E taking full advantage of them? (E needs to strike a balance between good working capital management and maintenance of supplier goodwill: very slow

payment will result in a poor relationship and could hinder E if it needs supplies urgently.)
5. Do E's suppliers offer discounts for prompt settlement? If so, what is the opportunity cost of not taking a discount?

Profit and loss account

Sales
1. Sales were budgeted to increase by 5 per cent. Was this increase to be achieved by a volume increase or by a rise in selling price or partly by each?
2. Sales targets have not been met. Why not?
3. How many different products are there?
4. What is the product mix?
5. Have any new products been launched in the current year? If so, how successful have they been?
6. Is any one product very dominant?
7. How price-sensitive is demand for E's products?

Direct materials
1. The cost of direct material has risen steadily in proportion to sales and is higher than the budgeted figure. What are the reasons for this?
2. Is E concentrating on the production of the more expensive lines?
3. What are the major raw materials used in E's products?
4. Have the prices of these raw materials increased?
5. Are they being used in greater quantities? If so, is this because raw material quality is poorer and wastage is higher, or are production problems causing wastage?
6. What methods of costing does E use?

Direct labour
1. Labour costs are currently budgeted to increase by 4 per cent and are at the moment slightly under budget. Is this because of a reduction in employee numbers?
2. Has there been a pay increase this year?
3. How do levels of overtime worked compare with budget and with previous years?

Contribution
(Contribution is the difference between sales and variable costs. For E to make a profit, contribution must exceed fixed costs.)
1. Why has contribution declined from 52 to 48 per cent over less than three years?
2. Is the company losing control over variable costs?

Overheads

Rates
Why have rates increased so markedly since last year? Is this the result of an

increase in the rate levied, or have E's premises expanded?

Maintenance
1. Why has an increase in maintenance costs been budgeted for? Why is it so high?
2. Does the maintenance expense in fact include capital costs? If so, an adjustment should be made.

Consumables
What consumables are used in the manufacturing process?

Finance charges
Does this include interest on the overdraft?

General expenses

Insurance
1. Why were insurance costs budgeted to fall in 1989?
2. They have in fact remained at last year's level. Why?

Legal expenses
Why were legal expenses budgeted to be below last year's level? Why have they remained the same as last year?

Selling and administration expenses

Salaries
1. Why have salaries fallen considerably?
2. Are there fewer salesmen?
3. Is the sales force currently under strength? If so, has this caused E's poor sales performance in 1989?
4. Has the remuneration package for salesmen been altered?
5. For instance, has basic salary been reduced and commission increased as a proportion of total remuneration?

Advertising and marketing
This has fallen significantly below budget and below the level in prior periods. The reduction in advertising and marketing expenditure may be the cause of the apparent fall in sales. If this underspend is the result of a deliberate policy, it should be reconsidered.

General

Management indicators
It may be appropriate to consider what indicators Parchment uses to evaluate the performance of E's management, and to consider how these have varied over the past three years.

Conclusion

As noted earlier, it would be dangerous to attempt to conclude on E's performance on the basis of the management accounts alone. At the planning stage of the audit, management accounts should be used, in the words of the auditing guideline, to

> add to the auditor's understanding of the enterprise ... [and] to identify, and thereby to enable the auditor to direct audit resources to, areas of the financial statements where the recorded values may vary from the values the auditor would expect.

Analytical review should be used at the planning stage to direct the auditor's attention towards areas about which more information is needed. It may well prove the case that many anomalies can readily be explained, but the auditor needs to follow up the leads, by discussion with management, further testing or more detailed review, in order to gain assurance on these points.

CASE 5   THE ENORMOUS ELECTRICAL COMPANY

Contents

The Enormous Electrical Company is undertaking its first stocktake. This involves counts both at the shops and EE's three warehouses. Students are required to evaluate both the warehouse stocktaking procedures and the audit work done on one warehouse.

Question 1 deals with controls over stocktaking, their purpose and the likely effects of their omission.

EE's instructions include the following controls.

1. The warehouse is tidied and goods are moved into separate areas, reducing the risk of double-counting or overlooking items.
2. Staff are assigned responsibility for areas. This again should reduce the risk of omission/double-counting.
3. Managers are told to look for obsolete and damaged stock.
4. Items are to be marked when counted, again reducing the danger of omission/double-counting.
5. Managers are to review the results of counts and investigate odd results. This should allow gross errors (e.g. miscoding) to be identified.
6. Cut-off details are to be noted as at 1 January 19X9. This will allow a subsequent check that items have been correctly included in/excluded from stock, according to the movement date, and that the corresponding debtor or creditor is correctly stated.

The instructions also contain a number of potentially serious weaknesses.

1. Stacking of cases will make it more likely that items are overlooked because counting staff cannot move freely and see all the merchandise. A related weakness is the failure to instruct staff to open boxes and check contents or to look for hollow squares.

2. Each area is counted by one member of staff only. Checks should be introduced – 100 per cent recount by another employee, supplemented by random checks by management – to reduce the risk of fraud or error. It would also be an improvement if at least some of the counts/checks were performed by people not normally responsible for the custody of stock.

3. Managers are not given any guidance as to the criteria for identifying obsolete or damaged stock. If this is left to their individual judgement, there will be big variations in practice throughout the company, and managers will be tempted to use the write-off as a balancing figure. Criteria should be explicitly stated, based on number of weeks without movement, stock code or description or any other appropriate basis.

4. Managers need to be told how to treat obsolete or damaged stock in their counts. Should it be excluded from the count completely or included at nil value or...? Treatment will be inconsistent if guidance is not given.

5. There is no provision for control over the issue of stock sheets. This presents the risk that sheets issued to staff counting at a warehouse may not be returned to the manager or that the manager may not return all sheets to head office. Either situation would result in the understatement of stock. Each warehouse manager should prepare an adequate supply of stock sheets before the count. These should be sequentially numbered and a note should be made of which staff member has received which numbers. After the count, the manager should check that all the numbers raised have been returned, either completed or blank, and any missing item should be followed up.

6. Arrangements for dealing with the movement of goods are quite inadequate. If goods must be moved between warehouses and shops over the year-end, EE needs to ensure that they are counted once and once only. As things stand, there is a risk that some items may be counted in the warehouse and again on receipt in a shop, and that others may be overlooked if the counters do not reach them in the warehouse and the shop count is finished before they arrive. Stocktaking arrangements should ensure that:
   (a) movements on 30/31 December are minimized;
   (b) items are counted at the warehouse before movement and boxes permanently marked, e.g. with stickers, to prevent double-counting;
   (c) goods received at shops from warehouses are segregated from other stock, again to avoid double-counting;
   (d) despatch note details for such goods are noted for subsequent follow-up.

7. Transfer of stock details from rough to final sheets presents the risk of misstatement as a result of omission, transcription error, etc. It would be preferable to omit this step and devote more resources to ensuring that the 'rough' sheets are legible. If rough sheets must be transcribed, control procedures should be introduced to ensure completeness and correctness, e.g. via use of batch totals.

In Question 2 students are asked to evaluate the adequacy of the audit work performed and make suggestions for improvement.

In addition to test counts, audit works should have included:

1. noting cut-off information for subsequent follow-up – this should have covered both deliveries in from suppliers and movements out to shops;
2. discussion of the manager's policy for identifying obsolete/damaged stock;
3. a note of the stock sheets used: as EE has not attempted to put the sheets under sequential control, the auditor should have tried to make up for this by, for instance, counting up the number of sheets being used;
4. as EE intends to transcribe the results from rough to final sheets, the auditor should make some arrangement for testing the transcription process.

The auditor has, quite correctly, carried out extensive test counts, comparing his results with the stock sheets written up by EE's staff. Unfortunately, his treatment of discrepancies between the two sets of results is unsatisfactory. Taking his notes on differences one by one:

Note (1): Does this mean that the damaged machine has been counted as if it were good stock? This is clearly an error and should be followed up.
Notes (2) and (3): Details of the movement of these items should have been taken, to ensure that they have not been counted again at the shop.
Note (4): The auditor should have confirmed the reason for the discrepancy, instead of assuming that it resulted from a stock movement.
Note (5): This seems to be a satisfactory explanation.
Note (6): In all three cases the actual stock is lower than the figure on the stock sheet. This could be because the storeman is either deliberately overstating stock, to conceal loss or theft, or because he is not a very accurate counter. In either case, the auditor should investigate further as there is a risk of systematic error in the whole area for which that storeman was responsible, and it may be that a complete recount is necessary. The fact that the items tested are low in value is irrelevant; the crucial finding is that the count was incorrect.

There appears to be a considerable risk of misstatement here, in view of:

1. the failure to control movements between the warehouse and the shops;

2. the lack of suitable procedures for dealing with obsolete/damaged stock;
3. the possibility of systematic error in part of the warehouse.

The audit work done has not been sufficiently responsive to these problems.

CASE 6 TECHNICAL WIZARDRY LIMITED

Contents

TW deals wholesale in typewriters and computer printers, which it buys from major manufacturers. It also sells computers. One computer, the T700, is imported ready-made to TW's design. The other, the T35, is manufactured by a TW subsidiary and is currently presenting a number of problems.

Students are asked to consider what stock valuation problems TW presents and then devise appropriate audit tests. The questions that need to be answered are:

1. Is stock stated at cost?
2. Is cost higher than net realizable value (NRV)?
3. Have adequate provisions been made in respect of slow-moving, obsolete and defective stock?

Taking each stock line in turn, problems and audit tests are as follows.

Typewriters and printers

Is stock stated at cost?
Cost is based on invoice price, and the stock history suggests that most lines will be at the most recent price, as the majority of stock is three months old or less.

The audit test could be a comparison of prices per print 006 with suppliers' invoices.

Is cost higher than NRV?
Cost seems likely to be below NRV, given the apparently buoyant demand and the speed at which stock is sold.

Comparison of cost with 19X1 sales invoice prices and current price lists should disclose any lines requiring write-down.

Have adequate provisions been made in respect of slow-moving, obsolete and defective stock?
The age profile according to report 004 does not suggest any problems here and the stocktake apparently did not disclose any obviously unsaleable items.

Probably no further audit work is required here, beyond discussion with management to establish whether there are any individual problems.

Spares

The aged analysis suggests that some typewriter and printer spares are over age and likely to be unsaleable. Different audit approaches will be needed for the more recent stocks — say three months old and less — and for the older items.

Is stock stated at cost?
Newer stock can be tested for pricing on the same basis as typewriters and printers. There is a risk that old stock may be incorrectly stated because the computer can deal with only three prices: the current one and the two previous ones. Audit tests will need to check that items with little or no movement are not being valued at inflated prices. This could be achieved by ascertaining the actual purchase price of older items by reference to invoices and comparing it with the price at which they are valued on the computer.

Is cost higher than NRV?
Again, newer stock is probably fairly low risk and can be tested by reference to price lists and invoices. Audit testing of older stock will need to cover the risk that stock is unsaleable and in need of partial provision or even complete write-off. Tests will need to be combined with those discussed in relation to the next question.

Have adequate provisions been made in respect of slow-moving, obsolete and defective stock?
In establishing whether stocks are obsolete etc., the auditor will need to cover the following ground.

1. By reference to the detailed 004 and 005 prints, establish which stock items are slow-moving by noting those which are in excess of, say, three months old.
2. Review sales forecasts and talk to responsible management to ascertain whether future sales are likely. Will prices have to be cut — and if so how far? — in order to sell items? Discuss whether any stocks are damaged or otherwise unsaleable. (This should have been revealed by the stocktake.)
3. Decide what items are likely to be unsaleable and by discussion with responsible management establish a basis for providing against them: e.g. write off in full, provide a rising percentage of cost according to age, etc.

The auditor will clearly have to rely on management to some extent in determining what level of provision is needed. Judgement will also have to be exercised in deciding how well founded management statements are.

T700 computers

Is stock stated at cost?
There is a potential problem here. The £ cost of T700s has fluctuated as a result of changes in the value of the RDR. TW proposes to use the average

rate in valuing the machines, but this may not be acceptable. It will be necessary to check the ageing of the stock by referring to the stock record cards in order to establish whether average cost approximates closely enough to actual cost. If it does not, for instance because the bulk of the stock was bought at the October rate, there will be a need to adjust.

Is cost higher than NRV?

Have adequate provisions been made in respect of slow-moving, obsolete and defective stock?

Audit work could be performed along the same lines as that on typewriters and printers to answer these questions.

T35 computers

Is stock stated at cost?

Cost of the finished machines, which were made by the subcontractor in Utopia, should be agreed to the supplier's invoice price.

Cost of work in progress should be based on actual materials, labour and overhead valuation, and audit tests should cover the following.

1. Agree raw materials prices and labour rates to supporting documentation (invoices, wages records).
2. Review the basis on which overheads have been allocated to stock value. This should be in accordance with SSAP 9, i.e. related production overheads.
3. Consider the possibility that abnormal overheads, relating to wastage in the first year, rather than normal costs of production, have been included in stock valuation. The auditor should review any available management accounts to ascertain whether such additional costs have been incurred and, if so, how they have been accounted for. Their inclusion in stock valuation would contravene SSAP 9 and present the risk that stock is overvalued.

Is cost higher than NRV?

Have adequate provisions been made in respect of slow-moving, obsolete and defective stock?

T35s made in the UK cost £2,850 each. Rectification costs are estimated at £250 each, a figure which should be reviewed by the auditor using information available about labour, materials and overhead costs. Selling price, according to the price list, is a maximum of £3,000, so that NRV is £2,750 (£3,000 − £250). Provision will have to be made to reduce the stock value of finished items to NRV. The auditor should also consider whether similar provision is needed in respect of part-completed stocks. Discussions with production management will be needed to establish at what point in production the defect requiring rectification has been occurring, and hence whether part-completed items include the fault and will need to be dismantled and reassembled.

The price list indicates that discounts are available on a rising scale on this line. Does this indicate that TW will need to cut selling price below cost in order to break into the market? The auditor should review sales budgets for 19X1 and discuss their implications with sales managers.

CASE 7   WAREHOUSEMASTERS LIMITED

Subject matter

Debtors: assessing a system and following up results of interim testing.

Contents

The case outlines a sales system and gives details of interim audit test results. Students are required to evaluate the impact of a number of weaknesses on the system and to decide how the final audit tests should be made responsive to these weaknesses. They are also required to interpret the results of a debtors circularization.

Question 1 is aimed at deciding what further audit work needs to be done. This can be considered under two aspects: those tests needed to establish whether the systems weaknesses have resulted in material error, and routine final audit testing.

Systems weaknesses are:

1. Test 3 indicates that ageing is not performed correctly. Cash which cannot be readily identified is posted against the oldest part of a balance. This is an incorrect procedure. Cash should be posted against the sales invoices to which it in fact relates. W's practice means that the oldest part of a debtor balance may be understated. This presents the risk that the credit controller may not be aware of accounts where older invoices remain unpaid, for instance because of a dispute, and will therefore not take the appropriate follow-up action. It also presents the danger that the auditor will overlook the existence of old items which may not be recoverable.

   The auditor will need to review all large cash receipts made in the last three months in order to establish whether misallocations have occurred and, if so, whether they have led to a material distortion of the '>90 days' debtors figure. The auditor should also report to management that the current allocation policy should be altered in order to prevent future misstatement.

2. Part (a) of Test 4 suggests that credit control procedures are by-passed on occasions. The commercial aspect, however, needs to be weighed against the increased risk of bad debts.

   There may on occasion be good commercial reasons for doing so — e.g. the wish to take advantage of a large customer order which may be forfeited by delay. The auditor should make a special review of the accounts of new customers who were not subject to checks on references in order to ascertain whether they include possible bad debts. This might be done by looking at old balances (if any) on such accounts and seeing whether payments are being received regularly.

3. Part (b) of Test 4 has revealed that the controller routinely overrides credit limits. This may be justified, but it would seem that additional audit testing of recoverability is required, in order to establish whether the credit controller has made correct decisions.

Final audit tests

The debtors circularization requires the following action.

1. Roll agreed balances forward to the year-end by verifying cash received, invoices issued and credit notes allowed against supporting documentation − bank statements, despatch notes, etc.
2. Follow up items not agreed. The differences noted on the Erica and Horrobin accounts appear to be timing differences, but should be checked in any case, to ensure that they have now been resolved. The Roberts balance should apparently be written off, and the status of any other retention balances reviewed.
3. Verify those balances not confirmed by means of the techniques suggested in 1 above. Recircularization is a possibility, but the short time available to complete audit work means that it may not be successful.

Other final audit work should include:

1. roll-forward of the total sales ledger balance between 31 August and 30 September, considering whether total figures for cash, invoices, credit notes, etc. compare reasonably with previous months;
2. comparison of cash received after 30 September with debtor balances at that date;
3. review of credit notes issued after 30 September to establish whether any of them cancels or reduces debtors included in the year-end total;
4. discussion with credit controller and management as to the recoverability of material old balances and the adequacy of the bad/doubtful debt provision;
5. reconciliation of the sales ledger control account at 30 September;
6. analytical review of aged debtors and bad/doubtful debt provisions at 30 September 19X7 and 19X6, and explanation of any major differences between the two years.

Question 2 considers the basis of the debtors circularization sample. Statement 3.901 is relevant here. The sample represents an attempt at representative sampling, but it should also have reflected some of the potential problem areas noted above − in particular new customers given credit without references and customers granted additional credit on the approval of the credit controller.

Question 3 is intended to provoke discussion. The auditors should report to management on the systems weaknesses noted. It is arguable, however, what these weaknesses are. Should W insist on references and preset credit limits if it risks losing customer goodwill by doing so? There is room for argument about the trade-off between internal control and commercial sense.

CASE 8   BRITLINGS BREWERY

Subject matter

Tangible fixed assets: identifying and evaluating controls and devising substantive tests.

Contents

The case outlines a fixed asset system and details of fixed asset values. Students are required to evaluate the system and suggest specific tests of balances.

Question 1 requires the evaluation of the system for controlling additions to and disposals of fixed assets.

There are in fact different systems for property, plant and fixtures and vehicles, and these need to be considered separately. In all cases, however, the overall objective is the same. Additions and disposals should be made only with authorization at a suitable level of responsibility. The sanctioning procedure should ensure that additions are within agreed expenditure limits, are of suitable assets and are accurately recorded in the accounting records. Disposals should be made in accordance with the company's policy and for a consideration which has been suitably authorized.

Property

The system of authorizing invoices subject to individual limits is only part of the overall control on spending. The main control over spending on property is via the system of sanctions and quarterly reports of expenditure. This should ensure that expenditure is incurred only as part of an authorized project and that overspends are investigated. The effectiveness of the system depends on the quality of the original budget − i.e. does it represent a realistic estimate of expenditure? − and the nature of the review carried out by the board. The point that needs to be made is that a report is, on its own, not a control. What is essential is that management notes and obtains explanations for major differences between budget and actual expenditure, so that errors or irregularities can be detected and corrected.

Disposals are controlled by the requirement for board approval and by the system of registering issues of property deeds. This second element, however, is again dependent on the use made of the register — i.e. if deeds are not returned, is their absence investigated?

Plant and equipment

The system of authority limits is the main control here. The plant register would act as a control if there were any system for ensuring that plant in the register is physically present. This could be achieved by conducting a cyclical inventory of plant so that all items were physically checked every three to five years.

Vehicles

The controls over vehicles are very poor. The fleet manager not only authorizes all purchases and sales but also keeps the registration documents. This would potentially enable him to buy and sell cars on his own account, as there is no evidence of outside scrutiny of the invoices he authorizes or the destination of the proceeds of disposals.

Question 2 requires students to suggest tests to verify existence and/or valuation of tangible assets. Their suggestions might include the following.

Existence and ownership of properties
1. Physical inspection of a sample of properties selected from the Estates Register. (This will provide evidence of existence, but not of title.)
2. Inspection of title deeds of properties selected from the Register, to ensure that they are in the company's name.
3. Locating any deeds booked out, to ensure that they do not reflect unauthorized disposals of property.
4. Checking additions/alterations from the Estates Register to source documentation, e.g. purchase invoices.

Property values fairly stated
1. Agreeing the cost/value of individual properties to the purchase invoice or the most recent surveyor's valuation.
2. Ensuring that any changes in value have been taken into account. These will include additions to the property, but also decreases in market value, e.g. because the trade at a particular pub has deteriorated.
3. In view of the company's accounting policy on depreciation of licensed freeholds, it is necessary to ensure that refurbishment is carried out to maintain the quality of premises. This could be verified by:
   (a) reviewing the level of expenditure in 19X9 compared with other years to ensure that the company is continuing to invest in refurbishments at a constant level;
   (b) reviewing and discussing budgets for refurbishment expenditure;

(c) ensuring by inspection of records that all premises have been refurbished within a given time span, e.g. every five years.

Existence and value of plant and equipment
1. Selecting items from the plant register and inspecting them.
2. Checking that costs in the fixed asset register agree with purchase invoices.
3. Checking the accuracy of the depreciation calculation in the fixed asset register

Existence and ownership of vehicles
1. Selecting a sample of vehicle registration documents and physically inspecting the vehicles to which they relate.
2. Selecting a sample of purchase invoices for vehicles and physically inspecting the vehicles to which they relate.
3. Extracting vehicle registration numbers from maintenance records, garage bills, etc. and ensuring by physical inspection, inspection of registration documents, etc. that the vehicles are in the possession of the company.
4. For a sample of vehicles selected from purchase invoices, registration documents, etc., check maintenance records for evidence of service having been performed.

(The tests for vehicles are designed to ensure that all vehicles purchased are owned and used by the company and not misappropriated, as would be possible, given the lack of supervision of the fleet manager.)

CASE 9   MRS BEETON'S KITCHENS LIMITED

Subject matter

Evaluating a purchases system and devising final audit tests of creditors and accruals.

Contents

The case gives details of a purchase ledger system and requires students to devise final audit tests of creditors and accruals. The system incorporates certain weaknesses which need to be taken into account in the audit testing.

Question 1 requires the student to draw conclusions from an interim test on purchases.

The test was designed to ensure that all goods/services received result in a liability being recorded in the purchase ledger. It was performed by tracing a sample of deliveries from delivery notes to the corresponding invoice and ensuring that the invoice appeared in the purchase ledger. The sample included a number of cases where the invoice could not be found or had not been posted. In some cases there appears to be a valid reason for this; in others there does not.

The invoice from Henry has been lost, and its absence was noted only when the auditor commented on it. This suggests a weakness in the system. There is no regular check on delivery notes or on the orders held in the purchase ledger department to ensure that old items for which a purchase invoice has not been received are followed up. It is therefore possible for invoices to be mislaid, leading to under-recording of liabilities.

It is acceptable for the Plastitops invoice to be held over until the dispute over price has been settled, provided that MBK makes an accrual for the amount that it considers is actually due to Plastitops.

There may be a good reason for the long delay in processing the PK Plumbing invoice: further information is needed. In any case, it will be necessary to check that an accrual has been made in respect of the goods involved.

The Lave-Vaisselle liability should be included in the accrual for goods received not invoiced, since it relates to goods received in the last two weeks of the financial year. Given that there is normally a four week delay in invoicing, MBK needs to ensure that all deliveries made by Lave-Vaisselle during June are accrued for.

The conclusion to be drawn from Test 2 is that there is a possibility of understatement of liabilities because:

1. there is no system for checking up on deliveries for which no invoice has been received within a reasonable period of time;
2. there is no system for ensuring that goods received more than two weeks before the year-end but not invoiced till after the year-end are accrued for;
3. purchase ledger balances are no longer compared with suppliers' statements. This is a 'long-stop' control which would compensate for the failure to follow up missing purchase invoices, as suppliers' statements would include such invoices and alert the company to the possibility that liabilities were understated.

It should also be noted that Test 2 relates only to items whose receipt is evidenced by a delivery note. It will therefore not reveal:

1. understatement of liabilities for services received;
2. understatement of liabilities for goods delivered if the delivery note has been mislaid.

Further audit work needs to be done to ensure that liabilities are not understated; it will be outlined as part of the suggested answer to Question 2 below.

Question 2 requires students to suggest tests of year-end creditor balances which will ensure that they are completely and correctly stated. These might include the following.

Purchase ledger balances

1. Circularize a sample of creditors to ensure that they confirm balances. This could achieve a high percentage coverage without requiring too many creditors to be contacted, given that seven balances represent 80 per cent of total purchase ledger value. It would probably need to be supplemented by other tests, given the likelihood that not all creditors will reply.
2. Reconcile balances as at July 19X9 with suppliers' statements and investigate differences (assuming that statements have been retained after November 19X8).
3. Review the file of stamped copy orders held by the purchase ledger department which have not yet been matched with invoices. Any which relate to deliveries prior to 30 June 19X9 should be investigated to ensure that they do not indicate mislaid invoices.
4. Obtain a list of managers entitled to authorize invoices and inquire of them whether they are currently holding any invoices which relate to goods/services received before 30 June 19X9 and which are in order for payment.
5. Ensure that any foreign currency liabilities have been translated into £ sterling at the year-end rate. MBK translates invoices at the rate prevailing on the day they are processed; this should be adjusted at the year-end, to reflect any exchange fluctuations since they were processed (e.g. the Ruritanian liability).
6. Reconcile the purchase ledger control account in the nominal ledger with the total of purchase ledger balances and follow up any reconciling items.
7. Review cash payments in July 19X9 to see whether they include any payments of liabilities existing but not recorded at the year-end.

See also 'Goods received not invoiced' below, as tests on creditors and accruals are closely linked.

Bank loan and bank overdraft

1. Obtain bank confirmation of the bank overdraft and loan balances at 30 June 19X9 via the standard bank confirmation letter.
2. Review the letter to ensure that it does not reveal the existence of any other overdrafts/loans which should be disclosed.
3. Reconcile cash book balance to balance per certificate, following up the treatment of reconciling items.
4. Ensure that MBK's overdraft and loans are within the limits sanctioned by the bank.

Goods received not invoiced

1. Review the invoices received by MBK between 1 July 19X9 and the

current date, and ensure that any relating to deliveries prior to 30 June 19X9 have been accrued for.

2. Perform an analytical review of purchase ledger balances and goods received not invoiced compared with purchases and stock in 19X9 and 19X8 and ensure that variations can be adequately explained. (NB: purchase ledger balances and purchase accruals need to be considered together in an analytical review. Delays in processing invoices in 19X8 compared with 19X9 may have resulted in a higher accruals figure and lower purchase ledger balances in that year.)

A test on cut-off based on the sequence of stock deliveries round the year-end would normally be suggested. This cannot be done here because MBK does not have a sequentially controlled record of receipts into stock based on pre-numbered goods received notes. Cut-off has been tested in item 1 above; it could also be tested as follows:

3. Check the dates of the delivery notes included in the goods received not invoiced schedule to ensure all receipts took place before 30 June 19X9.

4. By reference to the goods returned to suppliers book, ensure that any deliveries received prior to 30 June 19X9 which were returned to suppliers have been excluded from accruals.

CASE 10   GOLDEN FOODS LIMITED

Subject matter

Students are required to identify a number of areas which are likely to have an impact on a company's financial statements and to suggest strategies for dealing with them. Possibilities include: altering the accounts, qualifying the audit report, performing additional audit work and obtaining management assurance via the letter of representation.

Contents

The unresolved matters to be dealt with are:

1. The existence and valuation of the £18,000 stock at Wolverhampton;
2. The existence and recoverability of trade debtors totalling £535,000;
3. The recoverability of the £120,000 loan to Bartleby;
4. The correct treatment of the revaluation surplus and the capital commitments.

Effects on the financial results are potentially:

1. direct effect on profit if Wolverhampton stock is over- or understated;
2. overstatement of profit if debtors are overstated;
3. overstatement of profit if Bartleby loan in fact requires provision or write-off;

4. misstatement of additions to fixed assets, current liabilities and possibly also of reserve movements.

The auditors need to consider the impact of these items in terms of their materiality, and this will be discussed in the suggested answer to Question 2 below.

It needs to be stressed that there is no definitive answer to Question 2. The approach taken by the auditors will need to take into account a number of factors, including:

1. the auditors' assessment of materiality;
2. the time and the audit staff available;
3. the auditors' assessment of risk, which will be affected by their previous experience of GF's business and their impression of, for instance, the reliability of management estimates and forecasts.

A suggested approach is as follows.

Wolverhampton stock

Wolverhampton stock is stated at £18,000 (19X8—£39,000) out of total stocks of £140,000. The question not answered by the audit file is why the stock level has fallen so sharply. It may be that the 19X8 figure was in fact the anomalous one, but investigation is needed. If the correct figure were closer to the 19X8 level, this would imply a major (15 per cent) understatement of stock and hence of profit (10 per cent).

It is not the auditor's responsibility to perform stocktaking if the client does not do so, but the onus is on the auditor to form an opinion as to the truth and fairness of the accounts. The audit work already done is directed that way, but needs to be supplemented. Additional tests of the stock figure might include:

1. analytical review of stock levels throughout the year to establish whether the year-end figure is in line with trend;
2. review of wastage and write-off experience in prior periods;
3. roll-forward of the stock figure since the last stocktake to ensure that the year-end balance is consistent with the opening balance as adjusted for movements of goods in and out.

In addition, it is important that the letter of representation should make reference to the existence and valuation of stock at the depot. This is not intended as a substitute for audit testing, but rather as a reminder to management that they are responsible for the accounts.

Trade debtors

The audit work done on trade debtors appears to be appropriate and properly executed. The auditor responsible has, however, failed to follow up the test and use it as a basis for an opinion. The following additional steps need to be taken.

1. The auditor needs to ascertain and explain why there were timing differences in entering invoices and payments on fourteen of the balances circularized. Differences of a few days frequently occur because of postal delays and do not necessarily indicate any error or irregularity in processing. Long delays or anomalous differences (e.g. a receipt apparently credited to the account by GF before the date it appears in the customer's records) may be a sign of fraud or error and would require further audit work; but if timing differences are of the first kind, the reconciled balances can be treated as part of the 'agreed' figure.

2. The auditor needs to establish whether the dispute over damaged goods is an isolated incident, or a reflection of more widespread problems of delivery quality which may have resulted in debtor balances which are irrecoverable. In the former case, provision for the £3,000 in dispute would seem to be the most prudent approach, but the amount is not a material one, and failure to make provision would not affect the audit opinion.

   If the dispute is a symptom of problems, the auditor will need to consider the potential magnitude of its effect on debtors. Does the problem affect:
   (a) particular goods;
   (b) particular customers;
   (c) a specific delivery area?
   The auditor will need to quantify the possible effect, using understanding of the business and discussions with management, in order to decide whether the misstatement is a material one.

   It needs to be stressed that the auditor cannot simply note the possible existence of a problem. It is also necessary to quantify its effect in order to decide on further action. This is often difficult, as it requires the auditor to understand exactly why an irregularity has occurred and to judge whether it is the result of an isolated error or reflects an underlying systems weakness.

3. The auditor needs to do additional testing on the balances for which no reply has been received. Non-reply is a frequent problem in circularizations. Some companies cannot confirm a balance at a past date, because of the way in which they maintain their records; others simply ignore confirmation requests. A review of cash received and credit notes issued between the circularization date and the current date will indicate whether these debtors are settling their balances and also whether any balances shown as outstanding at the year-end are now irrecoverable.

If the results of these tests are satisfactory, it should be possible for the auditor to conclude that trade debtors are fairly stated.

The Bartleby loan

The £120,000 loan to Bartleby would, if written off, have a material effect on GF's profit for the year. The audit file does not at present contain enough information to allow an audit opinion to be formulated. The auditor needs to ascertain:

1. why no repayments have been received – this could indicate cash-flow problems on the part of the borrower, or might be in accordance with the loan agreement;
2. why GF does not wish Bartleby to be contacted. This refusal is not necessarily sinister, but certainly merits further investigation.

Further audit work should include:

1. obtaining answers to the questions above by means of discussions with suitably senior management;
2. reviewing Bartleby's most recent accounts in order to judge whether it is financially sound and likely to be able to repay the loan.

Because of the materiality of the loan, the auditors will need to be satisfied that it is likely to be repaid. Confirmation from Bartleby would be a valuable piece of audit evidence. If GF's management persist in their refusal to allow an approach, the auditor will need to decide whether the information and explanations received are satisfactory. He or she will certainly require the letter of representation to refer to the loan and the directors' belief that it will be repaid.

The auditor may decide that the audit report should refer to the loan. The nature of the reference will depend on the auditor's assessment of its recoverability. An emphasis of matter will be appropriate if and only if the auditor wishes to draw the reader's attention to the existence of the loan. In this case, it might run: 'Without qualifying our opinion above, we draw attention to the existence of an unsecured loan of £120,000 made by the company.' The emphasis of matter paragraph is purely a way of directing the reader's attention. It is not an audit qualification.

If the auditor is not satisfied that the loan is recoverable, it will be necessary to issue a qualified report. The qualification will be for uncertainty, not disagreement, unless the auditor has obtained any information that suggests that Bartleby will not repay. The amount of the loan makes it material but not fundamental to the company's results, and hence a 'subject to' qualification seems appropriate. This should set out sufficient detail for the reader of the accounts to understand the nature of the disagreement and its likely effects on the financial statements. The qualification might read: 'The company has made an unsecured loan of £120,000 to another company.

We have been unable to confirm that this loan will be repaid. Subject to this uncertainty . . .'

Additions to fixed assets

The overstatement of additions and creditors is simply an error and requires correction by GF. This should not create any objections on their part, as it will have no effect on profit.

Audit work needs to be done on the director's valuation of the land and buildings. The revaluation has been performed by someone who is qualified, but not independent of the company. The auditor cannot therefore place as much reliance on it as he or she would on a valuation carried out by an independent firm of surveyors. It is still, however, possible to assess the validity of the valuation by reviewing the basis on which it has been prepared in order to ensure that:

1. it is arithmetically correct;
2. it is based on reasonable assumptions;
3. it values the land and buildings on a basis comparable to and compatible with other similar properties on the market locally. Clearly, this is also an area where management should be asked to give assurance via the letter of representation that the revalued amount is a fair valuation.

If the auditor is unsatisfied with the results of the work done, he or she may have to request GF's management to obtain a second opinion from an outside specialist. If management is not prepared to do this, the auditor may find it necessary to qualify the audit report; it is not part of the auditor's duties to commission an independent report.

The auditor needs to ensure that a proper split has been made between the surplus arising on land and that on buildings, and that the surplus on buildings is being depreciated in accordance with SSAP 12.

The revaluation must be disclosed in accordance with SSAP 12 and the Companies Act. Disclosure must include:

1. both historic and revalued amount;
2. movement on revaluation reserve;
3. names and qualifications of valuers and the basis used;
4. the effect of revaluation on the depreciation charge.

CASE 11   MASSIVE MOTORS LIMITED

Subject matter

The case deals with a number of events and transactions which will not be fully resolved until after MM's year-end or which have occurred after the year-end but have implications for the financial results of the year. Such events and transactions will normally fall into the categories of commitments, contingencies or post-balance sheet events. Students are required to identify the relevant events and devise appropriate audit tests and accounting treatments for them.

Contents

The working papers disclose the following issues.

1. The June 19X8 revaluation of properties has disclosed an overall increase in property values, but reveals a £200,000 decline in the value of the Stoke garage (from £1,050,000 to £850,000), which is material in terms of the total value of property. As defined in SSAP 17, this is a post-balance sheet event.
2. The company has entered into commitments to:
   (a) purchase and build on a site at Newtown;
   (b) purchase a lorry, cars and various items of equipment.
3. IC's action against MM for damages represents a contingent liability. This may be offset by a contingent gain if MM succeeds in its case against Flitwick.
4. MM has a contingent liability in respect of the guarantee it has given in respect of its fellow subsidiary's bank borrowings.
5. The forward contract to buy dinars represents a commitment.
6. The warranty given in respect of car repairs represents a contingent liability.

MM's proposed accounting treatment/disclosure and the adequacy of the audit work done are considered below.

The property revaluation

Proposed treatment
MM does not propose to make disclosure of the revaluation, on the basis that it took place after the year-end. SSAP 17, however, includes in its examples of adjusting events 'a valuation which provides evidence of a permanent diminution in value'. As such, the drop in value would be required to be reflected on the face of the balance sheet and charged against revaluation reserve. The only grounds for treating this as a non-adjusting event would be evidence that the diminution in value had taken place after the year-end. In this case, it would be required to be disclosed by way of a note to the accounts, but the balance sheet value would not be altered.

If the drop in value is to be adjusted for, it will clearly be to the company's advantage to incorporate the full effect of the valuation into its balance sheet. In order to do this, it will be necessary to refer to the valuers to adjust the valuation back from the June to the March 19X8 level, although the difference is unlikely to be a significant one.

Audit work

The auditor will need to discuss with the valuers the basis on which the valuation has been arrived at, in order to determine whether the assumptions used in arriving at the valuation were reasonable and consistent with the previous valuation. In this case it is important also to establish whether the drop in value of the Stoke garage occurred before or after the year-end.

The valuer should also be asked to supply the auditor direct with written confirmation of the total value and its split between individual properties.

The purchase commitments

Proposed treatment

The commitments should be disclosed by way of note to the accounts. A distinction should be made between contracts for capital expenditure and expenditure authorized but not contracted for. Amounts would be:

	£000
Contracts for expenditure	775
Authorized but not contracted for	58

Audit work

Audit work should include inspection of the relevant contracts and board minutes.

The IC claim

Proposed treatment

MM currently proposes to offset the contingent loss on the IC action against the contingent gain from its case against Flitwick, and consequently make no disclosure in its accounts. It appears from SSAP 18 that this treatment is not satisfactory. The SSAP states (para. 6):

A contingency may be reduced or avoided because it is matched by a related counter-claim or claim by or against a third party. In such cases any accrual, or the amount to be disclosed in financial statements by way of notes, should be reduced by taking into account the probable outcome of the claim. However, the likelihood of success, and the probable amounts of the claim and the counter-claim, should be separately assessed and separately disclosed where appropriate.

The treatment recommended by SSAP 18 appears to be as follows. If the loss and the gain are both probable and equally probable and are expected to offset each other, it will be acceptable to disclose the situation by way of note, making separate disclosure of the loss and the gain, e.g.:

A contingent liability exists in relation to a claim for damages being brought against the company by a former customer. The company intends to bring a related claim against a supplier, both claims being for the amount of £280,000. In the opinion of the directors, it is unlikely that any loss will accrue to the company overall as a result of the two actions.

If the loss appears to be probable, however, and the gain a contingent one, the above treatment will not be appropriate. In this case, MM should make a provision of £280,000 in its balance sheet for the loss. The contingent gain may be disclosed by way of note because it is related to the contingent loss. (Note that a contingent gain not so related to a loss should not be disclosed.)

Audit work

The auditor needs to approach this situation with care because the degree of probability assigned to the loss and the gain will, as explained above, have a material effect on the company's profitability. Discussion of the current position with the company secretary is an essential part of the audit, but the following audit procedures should also be undertaken.

1. Contact MM's solicitors and discuss with them the likely outcome of the two cases.
2. Consider the need to obtain independent expert legal advice about the likely outcome of the two cases. (NB: If MM is not prepared to pay the costs of obtaining such legal opinion, it is not incumbent on the auditors to commission a survey.)
3. Review MM's contracts and other relevant correspondence with both IC and Flitwick.
4. Discuss with MM's operations manager and with the responsible staff at Bristol their views on the likely outcome of the two cases.
5. Review the basis on which the loss and gain have been computed and ensure that it appears reasonable.

In addition to work directed specifically towards the IC and Flitwick cases, the auditor should obtain assurance from the company's solicitors that no other legal matters exist which might affect the company's results. This should be done in the form of a request from MM to its solicitors, worded as follows:

In connection with the preparation and audit of our accounts for the year ended 31 March 19X8, the directors have made estimates of the amounts of the ultimate liabilities (including costs) which might be incurred, and are regarded as material, in relation to the following matters on which you have been consulted. We should be obliged if you would confirm that in your opinion these estimates are reasonable.

Matter: Action brought by Identical Copiers.
Estimated liability including costs: £280,000.

The bank guarantee

Proposed treatment
The guarantee to the fellow subsidiary's bankers should be disclosed as a note to the accounts: 'The company has guaranteed liabilities of a fellow subsidiary. The amount outstanding at 31 March was £1,500,000.'

Audit work
The auditor can confirm the existence of the guarantee by reference to the relevant board minutes, which should also be reviewed to ensure that no other guarantees have been given which require disclosure in the accounts. Massive Manufacturing should be contacted to confirm that the amount of the borrowing (and hence MM's contingent liability) has been correctly stated.

The forward contract

Proposed treatment
The bank letter provides adequate audit evidence of the forward contract.

Audit work
The forward contract to buy dinars represents a financial commitment and should be disclosed as a note to the accounts. No credit should be taken for the contingent gain on the contract to purchase dinars at £1 = 0.55 dinars.

The repair warranty

Proposed treatment
The company's proposed treatment of the liability is incorrect. SSAP 18 requires that 'a material contingent loss should be accrued in financial statements where it is probable that a future event will confirm a loss which can be estimated with reasonable accuracy at the date on which the financial statements are approved by the board of directors'. The amount of the warranty liability is a matter for discussion, but the company can reasonably expect that a liability will be incurred and should accordingly disclose the amount as part of the balance sheet figure for accruals.

Audit work
The audit file gives no indication of the likely size of the liability for repairs. As a first step, the auditor should quantify the potential cost to MM of carrying out its obligations. This could be done in a variety of ways. One possibility, for instance, is as follows. On average, MM has a liability for six months' sales, i.e. 750 cars. Using MM's average repair cost of £125 per car would give a liability of £93,750. This figure might be adjusted:

1. to reflect the amount of any known warranty claims currently outstanding;
2. to reflect the proportion of cars sold on which warranty claims have subsequently arisen.

This approach represents a fairly broad estimate. Depending on the circumstances, it might be preferable to look at the actual number of cars on which claims might be made, if there was a significant seasonal fluctuation in sales, or at the number of cars sold by the different garages, to establish whether any one garage has suffered significantly more or fewer claims than others.

CASE 12   HOLIDAY HOLDINGS LIMITED

Subject matter

Students are required to devise suitable analytical review procedures to audit hotel turnover and wages and salaries.

Contents

Estimated levels of income, wages and salaries

Income from room lettings
The information given allows the auditor to calculate what hotel income from room lettings should be, based on what is known about room charges and occupancy levels (rounded figures).

1. The number of room nights let was: $365 \times 100 \times 63\% = 23,000$.
2. The number of bed nights let was: $365 \times 200 \times 47.6\% = 34,800$.
3. The number of room nights for which rooms were let as doubles was: $34,800 - 23,000 = 11,800$.
4. Therefore the number of room nights for which rooms were let as singles was: $23,000 - 11,800 = 11,200$.

The estimated income from room lettings, based on these figures, is:

	£
11,200 @ £25	280,000
11,800 @ £30	354,000
	634,000

Wages and salaries
Park's expected payroll for the year can be calculated using the information given about actual pay for May 19X8:

Weekly staff:	£	£
May–July 19X8:		
13 weeks @ £3,000 per week	39,000	
August 19X8–April 19X9:		
39 weeks @ £(3,000 × 105%)	122,850	161,850

Salaried staff:
May–July 19X8:
3 months @ £4,580   13,740
August 19X8–April 19X9:
9 months @ £(4,580 × 105%)   43,281
                                                           _____
                                                           57,021
Pension contributions @ 5%   2,851   59,872
                                                           _____   _____
                                                                             221,722
Company's NI contribution:
10.5% × (£221,722 − 2,851)   22,981
                                                                            _____
Total expected payroll   244,703
                                                                            _____

Comparison of results

Income from room letting
The shortfall of actual room letting income compared with the estimate is £(634,000 − 622,710) = £11,290.
Reasons for this could include:

1. Discounts which have been given, for instance for block bookings or to regular customers, and which have not been taken into account by the audit staff in their calculations.
2. Misanalysis by the hotel accountant, which has resulted in the inclusion of room letting income as bar or restaurant sales. (The accountant is responsible for extracting this data manually, and there is no evidence from the audit notes that his work is subject to any check.)
3. Failure by reception staff to invoice all double occupancies correctly. They are required to check the status of the room as booked before preparing an invoice. If they do not do so, or if they fraudulently issue a single invoice (perhaps splitting the difference with the guest) the amount of room takings will be less than the occupancy figures, which are based on the booking data.
4. Other fraud or misstatement. If the accountant or other member of staff could devise a way to suppress invoices which had been issued and simultaneously to misappropriate cash takings, room turnover would be below the level suggested by the occupancy figures. A reconciliation of the type carried out here would be the only means of detecting this.

Wages and salaries
The difference between reported and expected payroll is:

	£
Payroll per financial statements	256,000
Expected payroll	244,703
	_____

Difference   11,297
                                                                    _____

The reasons for this difference may include:

1. A higher level of overtime for some or all of the year than for the first week in May, on which the expected figure is based.
2. The use of an incorrect number of employees in calculating the expected payroll figure. If there were more than fifty full-time employees at any point in the year, the expected payroll figure will be too low. Payments to casual staff should also be taken into account.
3. The payment of bonuses (e.g. profit-related or Christmas bonus).
4. Fraudulent 'padding' of the wages payroll. If the total payroll cheque is not compared with an itemized payroll summary showing the amount analysed between departments or individual employees, it would be possible to inflate the total figure and misappropriate the difference between the cash drawn and the amount needed to make up pay packets.

Advantages and disadvantages of analytical review

Analytical review has the following advantages as an audit technique.

1. It can ensure that audit effort is directed in the most efficient way by highlighting areas of possible concern.
2. It can save time by reducing the need for lengthy substantive tests. This is particularly beneficial where there is time or fee pressure.
3. Some types of analytical review, e.g. review of margins, sales per branch, output per head, can be closely related to the client's own management information and provide an additional insight into business performance.

The drawbacks associated with analytical review include the following.

1. Interpretation of results involves a high degree of judgement. This is particularly true where the auditor is comparing, for instance, results from two successive periods and needs to decide whether a given difference between them is significant. For this reason, it is dangerous, although tempting, to leave analytical review to more junior members of the audit team. They are able to produce analytical review calculations, but may lack the knowledge of the business needed to interpret them.
2. It is, similarly, often difficult for the auditor to evaluate management explanations of analytical review findings. These need to be handled with care, to ensure that they are an adequate account of all the facts.
3. Where analytical review involves making comparison between two sets of data, the results can be relied on only if one set of data has already been validated. For instance, it would be acceptable to use turnover levels as evidence that debtors are correctly stated only if the turnover figure has been tested by other means.

This is an objection to using comparison of current and previous year's results as the only audit test over a long period. If results continue to be misstated (by systematic fraud or error) in the same way, analytical review will not be effective, as the figures, though incorrect, will appear comparable. For instance, if payroll figures are systematically inflated by 10 per cent by a fraudulent employee over a number of years, comparison of two successive years will not show any anomalies.

CASE 13 FANTASY FASHIONS LIMITED

Subject matter

Audit reports; stock valuation.

Contents

Fantasy Fashions has suffered a serious setback. It manufactured T-shirts for Giant Stores, which rejected them on quality grounds. The managing director of Fantasy is now trying to make the best of the situation by including the T-shirts in year-end stock at £2 each − the selling price agreed with Giant. This clearly contravenes SSAP 9, which requires stock to be valued at the lower of cost and net realizable value. Students need to appreciate this point, as it is crucial to their decisions regarding further work to be done and the audit report.

Students are asked to consider:

1. *What further audit work should be done?*
   Stock value is overstated, and the audit report should quantify the effect of the overstatement. To do this it will be necessary to ascertain whether net realizable value is likely to be below cost. The auditor will need to estimate the likely selling price of the T-shirts, by such means as reviewing orders placed, price lists and other sales data and looking at the actual margin achieved on other finished goods sold.
2. *What should the wording of the audit report be and why?*
   By valuing stock at selling price, Fantasy is taking credit for a profit which will be realized only when the T-shirts are sold. Jim Green's arguments are irrelevant as far as the true and fair view is concerned. Students should redraft the accounts, using the 90p cost valuation for the T-shirts, in order to ascertain whether the effect of the overvaluation is material. A suggested revised set of accounts is given below.

Balance sheet at 31 December 1987

	£	Notes
Fixed assets	33,500	
Current assets		
Stock	22,698	a
Debtors	6,520	
Bank and cash	750	
	29,968	
Current liabilities		
Bank overdraft	5,000	
Trade creditors	9,675	b
	14,675	
Net current assets	15,293	
Net assets	48,793	
Represented by		
Share capital	10,000	
Reserves	38,793	
	48,793	

Profit and loss account	£	Notes
Turnover	181,640	
Costs	182,663	
Operating loss	(1,023)	
Interest	300	
Loss for the year	(1,323)	b

Notes
a   Stock now includes 19,500 T-shirts valued at 90p each.
b   Tax charged was on the profit for the year.

Students need to decide whether they are dealing with uncertainty or disagreement and whether the issue is material or fundamental to the true and
fair view.
   It is suggested that this is a case of disagreement rather than uncertainty,
as sufficient evidence is available for Pinkerton & Co. to make a reasonable
assessment of the cost/net realizable value of the T-shirts. The uncertainty
qualification would be used only in circumstances where information was not
available as the basis for an opinion.

The auditing standard states that disagreement/uncertainty is fundamental if it 'undermine[s] the view given by the financial statements taken as a whole'. Students need to decide whether the effect of the stock write-down is to undermine the impression currently given by the accounts. A case might be argued either way; the example given below assumes fundamental disagreement, on the grounds that the adjustment has the effect of converting the profit to a loss. Proponents of the view that the disagreement is material but not fundamental might argue that Fantasy remains a going concern, and that the unadjusted accounts still show a deterioration in results between 1986 and 1987.

Auditors' report to the members of Fantasy Fashions Ltd

We have audited the financial statements on pages ____ to ____ in accordance with approved auditing standards.

Finished goods stock has been valued at £39,000, which is the directors' estimate of its selling price. In our opinion, this stock should have been valued at the lower of cost and net realizable value, in accordance with Statement of Standard Accounting Practice 9. If stock had been so valued, the effect would have been to reduce the profit for the year by £21,450. In view of the significant effect of the overvaluation of stock, in our opinion the financial statements do not give a true and fair view of the state of the company's affairs at 31 December 1987, and of its result and source and application of funds for the year then ended.

Pinkerton & Co.
28 February 1988

CASE 14   BRIGHTER ALLOYS LIMITED

Subject matter

The case deals with a fraud which has been undetected by the auditors. Students are required to discuss the auditor's responsibility for detecting fraud and to suggest audit tests or other measures which might prevent fraud or ensure that it is detected.

Contents

The case describes a situation where a major fraud has gone undetected for a number of years, both by management and by two successive firms of auditors.

The first question requires students to discuss the extent of the auditor's responsibility for the detection of fraud. This is an issue that has aroused considerable debate. The public tends to take the view that auditors should accept a responsibility for fraud prevention and detection; the profession argues that fraud prevention is the responsibility of management. Fraud detection, according to this argument, is a by-product of the audit, arising from work done to ensure that the accounts give a true and fair view. Even if the auditor tests every transaction entered into by the company, there is no possibility of guaranteeing that fraud has not taken place.

So far, this appears to confirm Mark's view of the auditor's responsibility. Mark is, however, ignoring the fact that in this case material misstatement has resulted from the fraud. If, as seems implicit in the auditors' comments in Document 14.4, Brighter was given an unqualified audit report in 1987, their has been an audit failure. Could the auditors reasonably have been expected to detect the fraud? The guideline on engagement letters states that 'the auditor will endeavour to plan his audit so that he has a reasonable expectation of detecting material misstatements in the financial statements resulting from irregularities or fraud'. The guideline on fraud suggests issues which will be relevant to the auditor in planning the audit in order to determine how serious is the risk of fraud. Issues mentioned by the guideline which are relevant here, and which should have been considered by Parker & Co., include the following:

Business environment
– nature of the business, its services ... and its products.

Brighter's stock is largely high-value and relatively compact, and without specially opening drums and testing samples it is difficult to ensure that stock in hand is as described.

Control environment
...
– management's overall controls
– general segregation of duties
– existence and effectiveness of any internal audit function.

These are all factors that are lacking in Brighter's case. The auditors were aware that the control environment was a defective one.

Account areas
– susceptibility to fraud
– significance of each account area in the context of overall materiality.

Here again, stock clearly presents a significant risk.

The guideline also requires the auditor to consider the effectiveness of the internal control system if it is to be relied upon. Control aspects cited include:

– segregation of duties
– authorization
– completeness and accuracy of accounting data

- safeguard procedures
- comprehensiveness of controls.

Brighter's stock system showed deficiencies in all these aspects. It was completely dominated by Lodge, and, as is discussed in more detail in the answer to Question 2, it lacked suitable accounting controls. Where internal controls are weak or lacking, the guideline recommends that the auditor 'should take into account the possible effect of those weaknesses when planning his substantive testing'.

The audit work performed by Parker & Co. has not done this. They have tested the system in place at Brighter without considering whether it contains adequate controls. In fact, the system displayed a number of serious weaknesses.

1. There was no segregation of duties. Lodge controlled all aspects of stock, which allowed him to manipulate transactions in a number of ways. He could approve invoices from his accomplices in respect of non-existent or fraudulently described deliveries, as there was no independent check on the nature of deliveries or on the agreement of delivery notes and invoices.

2. Lodge wrote up the stock records. This allowed him to manipulate transactions by adjusting balances; the auditors tested receipts and issues to records, but any journal adjustments by Lodge were not scrutinized, so that fraudulent items would not be detected. In addition, there was no independent scrutiny of stock records to check that balances and movements were in line with expectations.

3. Lodge was responsible for stocktaking. The warehouse staff were not sufficiently knowledgeable to note any irregularities in his procedure, nor was there any independent check that the quantities which Lodge noted down as his stocktaking results were physically present. It was therefore possible for him to invent the results of the periodic stocktakes.

Despite the existence of these weaknesses, the auditors carried out tests of the system, implying that they intended to rely on it. This was to ignore the absence of controls. For instance, the test on receipts compares entries in the stock record with delivery notes. This test would be valid only if Brighter's warehouse staff made a check on all receipts to ensure that they corresponded with the delivery note description. The test on journal adjustments to stock was a check that Lodge had authorized all adjustments. Given that Lodge controlled the accounting for stock, it was unlikely that anyone else would be carrying out such adjustments. A more useful test would have been an inquiry into the reasons for adjustments. The auditors have in effect been testing procedures without considering whether they represented controls.

Given the absence of controls, the correct approach for the auditors to adopt would have been substantive testing, based on attendance at stocktaking. They did attempt this approach, but it suffered from the basic flaw that the auditor attending the stocktaking did not have an adequate understanding of the work to be done. As a result, he tested in one direction only – from the counts which Lodge had already carried out to the stock in hand. This gave Lodge the chance to manipulate the situation: the auditor was encouraged to test only those items whose book and physical quantities were in agreement. After the auditor had gone, Lodge could enter on the stock sheets details of the non-existent items he was using to inflate the stock figure. Limited test counts would be an appropriate audit strategy in a situation where other controls existed in addition to the stocktake. Here, the stocktake represents the only control: in order to obtain comfort, the auditor should have performed extensive counts in both directions – i.e. both from physical stock and from stock sheets – and attendance should have been so timed that the auditor was able to test the stock sheets in full, rather than testing those counts which Lodge had chosen to perform.

If the auditors had adopted the approach suggested by the auditing guideline, it appears likely that they would have detected Lodge's fraud before it was revealed by the 1988 stocktake – at least in the course of a thorough test of the 1987 stocktake. They had failed to respond to indications that a risk of fraud existed.

The second question requires the student to suggest measures which might have prevented or detected the fraud at BA, and to determine whose responsibility they are. There are numerous possibilities. The following suggestions cover the basic points.

Prevention

The main preventive measures here would have been the institution of accounting systems at BA which involved the segregation of duties. Given Lodge's senior position within the company, it would still have been possible for him to override controls, but other employees would have been aware of this fact. This might have presented a deterrent, or would at least have offered a real possibility that the fraud would be reported to management. The stock system should have incorporated the following features:

1. appointment of a warehouse manager with daily responsibility for the control of stock movements;
2. procedures for agreeing delivery notes from suppliers with the actual contents of deliveries;
3. stock records maintained independently of the warehouse manager and subject to review by senior management;
4. a system of sequentially numbered goods received notes raised by warehouse staff and used to update the stock records and support purchase payments;

5. a system of sequentially numbered issue notes raised by warehouse staff and used to update the stock records;
6. regular stocktakes carried out by a team of employees and supervised by someone who does not have daily responsibility for the custody of stock;
7. investigation and explanation of discrepancies between book and physical stock.

In addition, the purchases system should have included:

1. a requirement to support purchase payment requests with goods received note details, so that it was possible to link individual payments to the deliveries to which they relate;
2. control over amendments to standing data, so that new suppliers could not be added to the purchase ledger without the approval of the purchase ledger department. (This would have deterred Lodge from creating a fictitious company to receive payments on his behalf.)

These measures would have made it impossible for one person, single-handed, to manipulate the stock figure in the way that Lodge did. Collusion between two or more parties would have been necessary. The practice of encouraging staff to take their full quota of holidays, preferably including a continuous fortnight's break, would also ensure that there was some sharing of responsibilities, so that no employee's work could go unsupervised.

These controls should have been supplemented by a system for monitoring performance at group level, so that Lodge was reporting to Dickens on his performance on a regular basis via management accounts. In addition to this, a group the size of Dickens might have given consideration to the establishment of an internal audit department which could have performed tests as necessary on Brighter's systems. The internal audit department would have been well placed to carry out more detailed tests than the auditors would wish to carry out; this additional level of testing would have represented an extra safeguard against fraud or increased the chances of its prompt detection.

Detection

The discussion of Question 1 has indicated that the primary test which would have detected the fraud was a complete observation of the stocktake, including test-counts both from stock sheets to physical stock and vice versa and sampling of the contents of drums. Other tests which might have revealed the existence of part of the payments fraud would have been:

1. Vouching payments to suppliers to both invoices and delivery notes would have revealed the existence of any payments for which no goods had been received. (This would, however, have been a lengthy and time-consuming test, given the absence of any audit trail in Brighter's records

which might have allowed payments and other documentation to be linked.)

2. A review of newly opened purchase ledger accounts to ensure that they represent bona fide suppliers. This would involve a review of names and addresses and comparison with reference works such as local directories to provide confirmation of the supplier's existence. This would potentially have revealed the fraudulent nature of the payments made to the non-existent company set up by Lodge.

Responsibility

As the guideline makes clear, it is primarily the responsibility of management to prevent and detect fraud. The auditor's responsibility is limited to that of seeking assurance that material error has not occurred. It is therefore the responsibility of management to institute the controls described above with a view to the prevention and detection of fraud. The auditor has a responsibility, however, both to assess the risk of fraud and to design tests in response to that risk. It is also the auditor's responsibility to report to management weaknesses in the structure and operation of accounting systems and controls. This entails reporting both to the management of the subsidiary and to the holding company where the points made are of such importance as to be relevant to the holding company. Reporting to management by Slott and then by Parker would have highlighted the serious control weaknesses existing at Brighter and would have given the Dickens management an additional incentive to regularize the situation.

CASE 15   BANBURY GROUP PLC

Subject matter

The case presents students with the accounts of a company which is on the verge of failure, and requires them to consider the auditor's approach to such a company.

Contents

The first question requires students to identify those features of B's results which might have indicated to the auditor that the company was facing going concern problems. A variety of points might be suggested, especially with benefit of hindsight. The following are suggested, but students may identify others.

1. Turnover declined in 1986, despite the inclusion of Franklin's results for a full year.

2. Gross margin showed a sharp decline: it was 26 per cent in 1984 and 1985, and then fell sharply to 19.5 per cent in 1986.
3. The group's interest charges increased very markedly between 1984 and 1985 as a result of the need to fund the acquisition of Franklin. Total interest was £645,000 in 1984 and rose to £1,235,000 in 1985. This level reduced only slightly – to £1,229,000 – in 1986. This is disappointing in that Franklin might have been expected to start generating funds, thereby allowing the group to reduce its borrowings, during 1986.
4. The level of borrowings by the group rose sharply between 1984 and 1986. The rise in total borrowings is summarized below:

£000	1984	1985	1986
Bank loans	2,526	5,022	6,293
Other loans	195	437	768
Loans repayable in more than one year	1,375	2,715	3,222
Total	4,096	8,174	10,283

Total borrowings have increased by more than 250 per cent over the three years under review.

5. The increase in the level of stocks between 1985 and 1986, coupled with the fall in turnover, suggests the possibility that stock may not be readily saleable, e.g. because of defects or because the company has over-produced. Trade debtors also show an increase between 1985 and 1986, which is out of step with the fall in turnover. Is B experiencing problems with debt collection?
6. The funds flow statement emphasizes the deterioration in B's position. Over the three years summarized, funds from operations have declined until operations are absorbing rather than generating funds. By 1986 B is entirely reliant on non-trading activities for funds. An increasing amount of funds is being absorbed by loan repayments, which have risen more than fivefold over the period.
7. The chairman's statement made in August 1987 indicates other features of B's position which should have affected the auditor's view of the company. These include:
   (a) the failure of earlier, limited attempts to improve performance by disposing of unprofitable businesses;
   (b) the absorption of the rights issue proceeds in paying creditors;
   (c) the disappointing performance of Franklin, which was apparently acquired by the group in the hope of generating profits and hence boosting its flagging performance;
   (d) the transgression of the borrowing limits laid down by the articles of association and the debenture trust deed.

The trends noted above are all indications of possible going concern problems. B's position at the end of 1986 exhibits many of the symptoms of going concern problems which are listed in paragraphs 10 and 11 of the auditing guideline. The auditor therefore needs to consider what factors there are which suggest that the company will be able to continue in business despite its difficulties. These factors will include:

1. The directors' plans to overcome the company's difficulties: these should be specific and detailed plans for action and include a forecast of the likely effect of the planned action. It appears that B's directors have made such a plan, which involves the disposal of the US subsidiary and the Reading factory and the restructuring of Banbury Processing Equipment.
2. Confirmation by third parties that they intend to provide support for the planned action: in B's case the third parties whose co-operation is essential are its bankers and the purchasers of Franklin and of the Reading and Portsmouth factories. The auditor will need to see written confirmation of the bank's intended support; the existence of sales contracts will be adequate evidence for the planned disposals.
3. Professional advice obtained by the directors as to the company's situation: the directors, not the auditor, are responsible for obtaining advice from specialists where it is required, in particular about the legality of continuing to trade if insolvency is known.
4. Undertakings or guarantees between companies which are members of a group: the auditor cannot assume that one group company will assist another simply because assistance is needed. Has a legally binding undertaking been made, and is the other company in a position to carry it out?

The second question requires the student to determine the form which the audit report should take, based on the evidence available at the date the report was signed. What is crucial here is to determine whether, in the words of SSAP 2, 'the enterprise will continue in operational existence for the foreseeable future'. The auditing guideline defines the foreseeable future as 'a minimum of six months following the date of the audit report or one year after the balance sheet date whichever period ends on the later date'. This would here suggest that the auditor should take a view on B's going concern status for the period to 31 December 1987.

B's management has obtained the promise of support from its bankers, although on the basis that they may require repayment on demand. It has entered into agreements, subject to shareholders' approval, to dispose of the loss-making Franklin Corporation, and to improve liquidity by the sale and lease-back of two UK properties. In addition, it is attempting to improve its profitability by concentrating its manufacturing effort on profitable lines. These measures suggest that B's management is taking all possible steps to rescue the company. The form taken by the audit report will depend on the auditor's judgement of the likely effectiveness of these measures. Barnes and Hooi make a valid point here:

The auditor's role is to verify the fair presentation of the financial statements. This is still possible without qualification under the going concern concept, according to the auditing guideline, if the uncertainty is adequately disclosed and there is no likely impact on the carrying value and classification of assets and liabilities ... Clearly, going concern and failure prediction are different activities. The auditor is not required to forecast the company's future. Even if the failure were to occur within the 'foreseeable future' and the auditor had not qualified, he could still have acted within the guidelines provided he had exercised reasonable skill, care and caution.

(Barnes and Hooi, 1987, pp. 32–3)

Barnes and Hooi go on to make the point that the current auditing guideline places too much reliance on the auditor's subjective judgement. This is debatable; it is clear, however, that the current guideline does not require the auditor to attempt to predict the future. What it does require is that the auditor should make a fair judgement based on the information available. Under this approach, the auditor would be justified here in producing an audit report with a 'subject to' qualification, as set out below:

Report of the auditors to the members of Banbury Group plc

We have audited the financial statements on pages —— to —— in accordance with approved auditing standards.

The company's principal UK subsidiary, Banbury Processing Equipment Ltd, has been granted continuing facilities by its bankers upon normal banking terms subject to reduction in line with an agreed asset disposal programme and confirmation of a continuing recovery. The company is in breach of its borrowing powers under the debenture trust deed securing the 9% Debenture Stock 1989–96, which gives the debenture holders the right to demand repayment. As stated below, proposals to rectify the situation are currently under negotiation. The financial statements have been prepared on a going concern basis which assumes that these negotiations will have a successful outcome.

In our opinion, subject to the continuing support of the company's bankers and debenture holders, the financial statements, which have been prepared under the historic cost convention, give a true and fair view of the state of affairs of the company at 30 November 1986 and of the loss and source and application of funds for the year then ended and comply with the Companies Act 1985.

The report indicates to the reader of the accounts the two main issues on which B's survival depends and makes clear that the going concern basis has been used to value assets. It is open to students to suggest an alternative report. A case might be made for an 'except for' or adverse report – but supporters of this view would have to be able to put forward a strong argument against B's viability. As the auditing guideline stands, it appears to give the auditor discretion in deciding what constitutes a reasonable likelihood of going concern status.

Bibliography

Accounting Standards Committee (1989) *Accounting Standards 1989/90*, The Institute of Chartered Accountants in England and Wales, London.

Auditing Practices Committee (1989a) *Auditing and Reporting 1989/90*, The Institute of Chartered Accountants in England and Wales, London.

Auditing Practices Committee (1989b) Auditing Standard − The Audit Report, *Accountancy*, April, pp. 167−72.

Auditing Practices Committee (1990) Auditing Guideline − The auditor's responsibility in relation to fraud, other irregularities and errors. The Institute of Chartered Accountants in England and Wales, London.

Barnes, P. and Hooi, D. (1987) The strange case of the qualified audit report, *Accountancy*, November, pp. 32−3.

Coopers & Lybrand (1985) *Student's Manual of Auditing*, 3rd edn, Gee & Co, London.

Easton, G. (1982) *Learning from Case Studies*, Prentice-Hall International, London.

Gray, I. and Manson, S. (1989) *The Audit Process*, Van Nostrand Reinhold, London.

Hatherley, D. J. (1980) *The Audit Evidence Process*, Anderson Keenan, London.

ICAEW (1979) *Guide to Professional Ethics*, revised 1985 and 1987, The Institute of Chartered Accountants in England and Wales, London.

Lee, T. (1986) *Company Auditing*, 3rd edn, Van Nostrand Reinhold, Wokingham.

Sherer, M. and Kent, D. (1983) *Auditing and Accountability*, Paul Chapman, London.

Woolf, E. (1990) *Auditing Today*, 4th edn, Prentice-Hall International, London.